F.X. Feeney / Paul Duncan (Ed.)

ROMAN POLANSKI

TASCHEN

KÖLN LONDON LOS ANGELES MADRID PARIS TOKYO

FRONT COVER
Still from 'The Pianist' (2002)
Wladyslaw Szpilman (Adrien Brody) is saved from
Auschwitz because of his genius as a musician.

FIRST PAGE
On the set of 'Repulsion' (1965)
Polanski, focussed, intent, typically out of his chair.

FRONTISPIECE
Still from 'The Tenant' (1976)
A study in alienation, well framed by Sven Nykvist.

THIS PAGE
1 **On the set of 'The Tenant' (1976)**
Polanski, coordinating with actress Dominique Poulange.
2 **On the set of 'Frantic' (1988)**
Plotting literal suspense, atop illusory Paris rooftops.

OPPOSITE
On the set of 'Oliver Twist' (2005)
Training a ready eye on a kindred young survivor.

BACK COVER
On the set of 'The Pianist' (2002)
Roman Polanski.

Images

Roman Polanski, Paris: 2, 4 (2), 6, 9, 14, 15, 18, 20 (2), 21
(2), 22 (2), 23, 24, 25 (2), 27 (3), 28 (2), 30, (2), 31 (2),
32, 33 (3), 34 (2), 35, 36 (2), 38 (2), 39 (2), 40, 41 (2),
42, 43, 44 (2), 45, 46, 48, 50, 51, 53, 54, 55, 56 (2), 58
(2), 59, 60, 61, 62, 64, 65, 67, 68, 70 (2), 72, 73, 75, 76
(2), 79, 80, 82, 84 (2), 85, 88, 89, 91, 92, 93, 94, 95 (2),
96 (2), 97, 100, 101, 105, 109, 110 (2), 111, 112 (3),
113, 120, 124 (2), 125 (2), 126, 128, 129, 130, 133, 135,
136, 138 (2), 139, 141, 142, 145 (3), 146 (2), 147, 148
(2), 150, 151, 154 (2), 155 (2), 156 (2), 157 (2), 160, 161
(2), 162, 163, 164, 166, 167, 168, 170 (2), 172, 174,
175, 176, 186, 190, 191
British Film Institute Stills, Posters and Designs, London: 1,
17, 20, 21, 23, 24 (2), 32 (2), 37, 40 (2), 49, 50 (2), 51,
52, 53, 56, 57, 59, 63, 66, 68, 71, 74, 75, 76, 79, 85 (2),
86, 88, 89, 99, 106, 109, 116, 117 (2), 118, 119 (2), 121,
122, 123, 129, 152, 186, 187 (2), 190
Photofest, New York: 52, 80, 81, 102, 104, 120, 127 (2),
152, 153, 158
PWE Verlag / defd-movies, Hamburg: 17, 21, 44, 116, 132,
134, 139, 140, 141
Joel Finler Collection, London: 12, 57, 68, 69, 78, 90, 98, 107
The Kobal Collection, London/New York: 84, 87, 91, 104, 107,
118, 159
Guy Ferrandis/H&K, Paris: Front Cover, 5, 178, 180 (2), 181,
182, 183 (2), 184 (2), 185 (2), Back Cover
CORBIS: 114 (Douglas Kirkland), 140 (Etienne George), 148
(François Duhamel)
Cahiers du cinéma, Paris: 108 (Coll. cdc/D. Rabourdin)
F.X. Feeney: 8, 10, 192

© 2006 TASCHEN GmbH
Hohenzollernring 53, D–50672 Köln
www.taschen.com

Editor/Picture Research/Layout: Paul Duncan/Wordsmith Solutions
Editorial Coordination: Martin Holz, Cologne
Production Coordination: Ute Wachendorf, Cologne
Typeface Design: Sense/Net, Andy Disl, Cologne

Printed in China
ISBN 3-8228-2542-5

To stay informed about upcoming TASCHEN
titles, please request our magazine at
www.taschen.com/magazine or write to:

TASCHEN America,
6671 Sunset Boulevard, Suite 1508,
USA-Los Angeles, CA 90028,
contact-us@taschen.com,
Fax: +1-323-463.4442.

We will be happy to send you a free copy of
our magazine which is filled with information
about all of our books.

CONTENTS

An Orphan of the Storm
1933–1946

9 Komorowskiego, Kraków (2004)
The first house Polanski remembers, fittingly
emblazoned with a creature of the imagination.
Roman lived here from ages 4 to 7, his few
blissful years as a child.

"All this talk about my past. I realize that, as a
child, all those things seemed natural to me. I was
living them. But sometimes, recently, I wake up at
night. I am forced awake because I am reliving
these things. I sort of stand back and look at them
as an outsider. You know, I think it has been an
amazing life, and hardly worth it, as a matter of
fact."

Roman Polanski

One day in 1946, staffers at a radio station in Kraków, Poland found themselves
playing host to an inquisitive teenager so small he looked seven years old. One of
the staff, a Communist theatre official named Maria Billizanka, quizzed him about
his interests as if humouring a small child. She learned he was not only 13, but
tough, self-assured and intelligent. He told her the kids she was using on the air
sounded phoney. She challenged him to do better – right here, right now. The boy
sprang into a campfire performance he had perfected the summer before. It was the
monologue of a shrewd old man, done in an expert country accent. His self-taught
changes in voice and body language were so calm and confident that Billizanka
offered him an acting job on the spot.

Ready curiosity, brash honesty and uncommon talent – what a fitting start to the
career of Roman Polanski. At age nine, he had seen his parents taken prisoner by the
Nazis, and, having narrowly escaped capture himself, survived into his early teens by
hiding out in the Polish countryside under a false name. Europe was full of hard-luck
children at that time. Billizanka and her colleagues must have met more than their
share – but this one had a rare resiliency, a sunny unbreakable spirit.

Polanski had been born in Paris, France on 18 August 1933; mere months after
Hitler came to power. His parents were both of Jewish descent, though his mother's
family had converted to Catholicism a generation back. Feeling themselves at risk,
they moved back to their native Kraków while Roman was still an infant. This seems
an awfully perverse move in retrospect. Poland was shortly to become the infernal
heart of the impending holocaust, but no one outside of Hitler's inner circle could
imagine what was really in store. Polanski's father reasoned that Kraków's
friendliness toward Jews, dating back to the reign of King Kazimierz in the Middle
Ages, made it the best refuge against the anti-Semitism boiling over everywhere else.
For a time, this proved correct. As recounted in his 1984 autobiography, Polanski's
earliest memories of Kraków abound in moody beauty and magic. Over the front
door at 9 Komorowskiego there was (and remains to this day) a heraldic bas-relief of
a mythical creature, half-lion, half-dragon. The third floor landing outside his
parents' apartment was a shadowy playground for his early imagination to run wild
in. His mother's tender, enigmatic nature was another important legacy. No photo
survives of her, but later Polanski would consciously recreate certain particulars of
her sensual elegance in Evelyn Mulwray, the doomed heroine of *Chinatown* (1974).
Indeed, the fresh vividness with which the furniture, clothes and atmospheres of the
1930s are evoked in that film has the intensity of a childhood memory. Polanski was
just six when the Nazis invaded Poland in September 1939. What followed was, at
first, uneventful. 'The Germans' method was to lull people into passivity,' he later
wrote, 'to foster a sense of hope, to persuade the Jews that things couldn't possibly
be *that* bad.' He would be nearly 70 years old before he could recreate what he had
seen on film, combining the nearly identical experiences of musician Wladyslaw
Szpilman with his own observations in *The Pianist* (2002) to show precisely how,
step by step, the Nazis psychologically cornered their victims. For Polanski and his
family, there were 'ominous turns of the screw'. Public schooling was terminated for
Jewish children. Typewriters were confiscated from Jews, then fur coats. Polanski,
his parents, and his older sister Annette were shortly relocated in a ghetto across the
river Vistula. To visit this place today is to be startled by how small it is. The Nazis
built only one wall. The ghetto was sealed in by an abrupt hill topped with barbed
wire at its back, and the steep levee of the Vistula curving along its flank. From an
early age, Polanski became adept at slipping through these barricades and wandering

the city outside. His father encouraged his self-reliance. The boy could pass for a gentile because he had inherited his mother's blond hair and upturned nose. For a time, both parents had permits which let them work outside the ghetto. Thus they established a network of sympathetic contacts throughout the city, and taught young Polanski what to do and say should he ever find himself on his own.

'I realized why the street had emptied so quickly,' he wrote of an atrocity he witnessed at this time, one that later informed the violence in *The Pianist*. 'Some women were being herded along by German soldiers. Instead of running away like the others, I felt compelled to watch. One old crone, at the rear of the column, couldn't keep up. A German officer kept prodding her back into line, but she fell down on all fours, grovelling, whining and pleading with him in Yiddish. Suddenly a pistol appeared in the officer's hand. There was a loud bang, and blood came welling out of her back. I ran straight into the nearest building, squeezed into a smelly recess beneath some wooden stairs, and didn't come out for hours.' As an artist, Polanski understandably resists all readymade analyses of his work based on such early blows to his psyche. 'Rather, I feel that my escapades, my wildness and strength have sprung from a sense of wonder at what life has to offer.' Yet what he lived through so young inevitably shaped him. Forbidden by the Nazis to learn to read, he became an insatiable movie-goer, peering for long hours at night through a gap in the ghetto wall at the newsreels and features which were projected against the open-air screen in Podgorze Square. 'Only pigs go to the movies', read a bit of graffiti frequently scribbled by the Jewish resistance. 'Jews = lice = typhus' were words Polanski could only dimly make out with his patchy reading skills, from one propaganda newsreel. But for a small child actually living behind barbed wire, even a film choked with the most toxic anti-Semitic trash promised a bright escape from where he was in reality.

A more vital escape, the most fateful of his life, commenced at dawn on 13 March 1943. The Kraków ghetto was about to be liquidated. For weeks, there had been frequent raids by the Gestapo. Polanski's mother was arrested while returning to the ghetto from work, her permit in hand. "Don't cry, people are watching," Polanski warned his weeping father, for they were also at that moment outside the ghetto, on the elder Polanski's permit, when they received the news. He was frightened that his father's tears would signal that they were Jews to the Kraków gentiles passing them on the street. 'There was no doubt in my mind [then, that my mother and I] would be reunited,' he would later remember. So it was, at dawn, that his father quietly walked Polanski to a spot just out of the sentry's sight at Podgorze Square, clipped the barbed wire, hugged him and bid him to run. A long adventure ensued. At first Polanski lingered, watching the ghetto's destruction. He even tried to approach as his father was force-marched with other prisoners toward the waiting trains. "Shove off," his father mouthed angrily, and this time he obeyed. His parents had provided a Catholic family called the Wilks with money to keep him, but they farmed him out to the Puteks, who were likewise jittery. Young Polanski was a handful. He talked the Putek's boy into pretending they were Germans, to get better seats at a movie matinee – a stunt that could have landed them both on a train to Auschwitz. One day, when Janka, a pretty 19-year-old relation of the Puteks stopped by, Polanski annoyed her – first with his incessant hammering (he was trying to build a movie projector), later with his pranks at the flat's doorbell. "Turn the little bastard in," was her advice to her relatives. The Puteks instead arranged for her to take him deep into the countryside, 40 kilometres to the south of Kraków, to a tiny village called Wysoka. There, the Tatras mountains, blue and massive, form a

ABOVE
On the set of 'The Pianist' (2002)
A battered but unbroken Star of David, upon a kiosk coated with Nazi pamphlets and propaganda.

PAGES 6/7
On the set of 'The Pianist' (2002)
Happiness is fleeting. History abounds in horrors. Art prevails.

Wysoka, Poland (2004)
Polanski took refuge at age 9 in a hut no longer standing, at left. Unpave that road, and hear the sleigh bells of Professor Abronsius approach, to the music of Krzystof Komeda.

"It's a strange talent, you know, to be happy. Many don't have it. But he was always full of good spirits. I never saw him melancholy."
Did he ever speak of the war?
"Never. Perhaps there was a bit of that syndrome in him. 'Well, that's over. Now let's be happy.'"
Agnieszka Osiecka,
Lodz classmate, later Poland's most popular lyricist and poet

snow-capped wall to the south. Perspectives there shift playfully, amid rolling farms and sudden cliffs. Polanski got off the train at Przytkowiece (whose depot stands to this day, a relic of the Austro-Hungarian Empire) and hiked the rugged 15 kilometres, mostly uphill, to the ramshackle cottage where the Buchala family would put him up for the next two years.

'I still missed my parents dreadfully,' he later wrote, 'And this, my third move in as many months, should by rights have aggravated my gnawing sense of depression. It was the countryside that saved me... I was discovering a new world. It was like starting life afresh.' He led the life of a farm boy, milking cows, driving cattle to graze. The Nazis would still sweep through the area searching for Jews from time to time. A German soldier once shot at him for sport as he crossed a field picking blackberries, forcing him to lay low in the deep grass until nightfall – but on the whole, Polanski was now safer than he had been.

Landscape is an often overlooked fundamental in the shaping of individual personalities, especially creative ones. Well and good to say a given artist suffered this or that, was too poor or too rich, had a mother or father who either too lavishly indulged them or too damagingly opposed them, that they endured daily life under the Nazis or Ku Klux Klan, or outgrew the petty sexual and theological bigotries of small-town life the world over. Anger about suffering and injustice inevitably beget an artist's early themes. But what is the landscape that forms this person? What is the physical experience of nature, of the elements, of earth and sky that turn the inner, poetic compass-needle of his or her imagination as it develops? Vladimir

Nabokov noted that even late in life, in his nightly dreams, he could often discern the forest trails of his family's estate in northern Russia, which he had not seen in person since he was 16. These settings were so at home in his slumbering brain that he would often fail to notice them, free as they were of any nostalgic emotion in his nocturnal imagination, and distracted as he had been by the dream's foreground action. Yet, there they were. Wysoka seems to have had this effect on Polanski, forming an imaginative pattern in his adult work as explicit as a watermark. This is particularly true of the surrounding terrain, with its long-range views and layered horizons. His people often approach from great distances when we first meet them. (*Two Men and a Wardrobe*, *Mammals*, *Cul-de-Sac*, *The Fearless Vampire Killers* and *Pirates* all begin so.) Or, we confront a congress of mysterious horizons, be they misty triplets of hills beyond hills (the first shots of *Macbeth* and *What?*), ocean waves (from which we retreat through a staring ship's porthole in *Bitter Moon*), a highway stretching to the vanishing point (*Frantic*), or a jumble of cityscape rooftops viewed from celestial heights (*When Angels Fall*, *Rosemary's Baby*). Polanski will use the tensions latent in whatever topography is under scrutiny to tease our curiosities, the deeper to involve us in this or that story. The sentry's question "Who goes there?" is the primitive suspense he habitually invokes. He must have done a lot of looking and wondering in those long days at Wysoka. Those specks approaching from the horizon might be Nazis, come to kill him at last, or they might be saviours, come to tell him the war is over. Which? Either way, he trained his gaze early, not merely to be watchful, but vigilant.

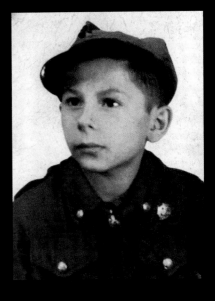

Roman Polanski (circa 1946)
It was as a Boy Scout that Polanski (still using his refugee surname, Wilk) discovered he had acting talent, performing a solo campfire skit as an elderly, catastrophe-prone mule driver.

By early 1945 the Nazis were in retreat and so Polanski was sent back to Kraków. He spent the last days of the war hiding in an air-raid shelter. By the time chance reunited him with his father several months later, he was used to living on his own. This suited his father, who following his own liberation had met another woman, Wanda. Polanski's mother was dead. Wanda did not want anything to do with the children of her new husband's previous marriage (Annette had also survived, and moved to Paris), so Polanski was given an allowance, a tutor to fill in his long-overlooked schooling, and a room of his own in a boarding house.

For a brief time, he thought of himself as a Catholic. His foster-mother back in Wysoka, Mrs Buchala, had been deeply religious in a way free of superstition or the itch to judge others. Hers was a faith to which the boy freely gravitated, praying as he did with a child's simplicity for his mother to be safe. However, the crushing knowledge of his mother's death finally divorced young Polanski once and for all from any religious faith. Prayer had proved fruitless. The universe was governed by chance, and any notion of 'a life to come' was a pathetic and absurd refusal to face and master this life, here – such was Polanski's raw new philosophy. Although he was to refine this with a searching intellect and salty humour in the years ahead, he would never waver from this youthful, self-taught stance.

Such was the stubborn ferocity of spirit that faced Maria Billizanka at the radio station, when she mistook this upstart for a small child and found herself launching his career.

**Crashing the Party
1947–1957**

"We were teenagers, just after the war, when I first met Roman," recalls cinematographer and author Kris Malkiewicz. "He was still called 'Roman Wilk', but he was already well known as a child actor, because he'd been in a very successful play called *A Son of the Regiment*." Malkiewicz and Polanski became lifelong friends at the Kraków YMCA, where they had gone to hear a clandestine jazz concert. As he now recalls with a fond smile, "Roman had a reputation for being this obnoxious brat who was somehow everywhere." Billizanka had cast Polanski in a Marxist radio show, *The Merry Gang*, and given him that plum title role in *A Son of the Regiment*. This won the attention of the talented students at the Film School in Lodz, among them Andrzej Wajda – who later invited him to play a memorable young tough in his debut feature, *A Generation* (*Pokolenie*, 1953), an intricate tapestry of wartime teen-life whose smash success abroad established Wajda and paved Polanski's entry into the directing program at Lodz in 1955.

For the near-decade between the war and his admission to film school, Polanski soaked up life as an actor, athlete and art student. When he wasn't performing, he was pumping older actors and technicians for everything they knew about their respective crafts, bicycle racing (a sport he pursued with singular passion), chasing girls and sponging up fresh knowledge about the visual arts. He developed a voracious appetite for Shakespeare as well as for the flood of American and western-European films that were now reaching Poland after years of eclipse – musicals, thrillers, adventure films, crime pictures. (His favourite film was *Odd Man Out*, Carol Reed's stylish 1946 thriller about a fugitive.) His world still abounded in odd dangers. At 15 he was almost murdered. A seemingly friendly teen (already being sought for several other killings) lured him into an abandoned bunker on the pretext of selling him a racing bike, and opened a near-fatal gash in his head. (The boy was hanged after his arrest.) Polanski then dodged a stretch in the army – ignoring the summons, wandering the countryside for long months, keeping no fixed address, until one day he discovered that by a miraculous fluke, his papers had been misplaced. 'I was a nonexistent person to the government,' he later exulted.

He was certainly no non-person at Lodz, where an elegant 19th-century mansion had been revamped to create a film school. The rigorous training included a year of

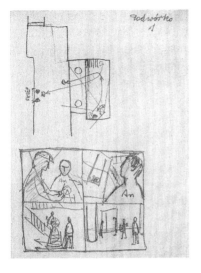

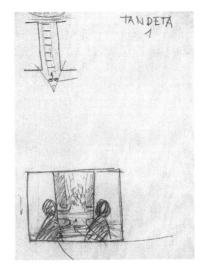

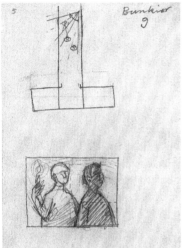

still photography. He agitated to skip this part (he had learned a lot on his own, playing with friends' cameras), but his teachers insisted. However much he thought he knew, Polanski later gratefully realized that being forced to concentrate all of his expressive powers into single images was useful preparation for the next step. There were also enormous technical benefits. In Hollywood, he would become legendary at film laboratories for stopping by with a thermometer to personally take the temperature of the vats in which his footage was to be processed. This may have been more symbolic than anything – a way of warning technicians, 'I know what I'm doing, and I know what you're doing, too.' But it reflects an earned expertise.

The eight 35-millimetre short films Polanski completed between coming to Lodz and directing his first feature likewise form a striking body of work in miniature. He arrived at film-making in command of so much theatrical craft and raw experience of life, in addition to his talent, that even his minute-long student exercises are still riveting to watch.

Polanski's film career started with a stutter. In 1955 he shot a short colour film in Kraków that dramatized Polanski's near-death at the hands of a serial killer, but much of *The Bicycle* was destroyed in the laboratory and so never completed. The

first film to be completed, *Murder* (*Morderstwo*, 1957), tells its 'story' in three simple, atmospheric shots. 1) A door latch, seen in tight close-up, opens to admit a stealthy figure into a darkened room where another man lies sleeping. 2) The intruder's hands plunge a knife-blade into the sleeper's chest and then muffle his outcry. 3) The killer turns, his black trench coat, hat and pinched, piggish face briefly evoking (in the blink of an eye) a Nazi or a secret policeman until he once again becomes an anonymous, shadowy mass and lets himself out the way he came in – leaving us where we began, staring at the door latch in close-up.

This film may not be much – it is just an exercise. Yet these three quick shots are each so charged with suspenseful detail that they honourably raise the curtain on the body of work to come. Even its shape, in under a minute, is pure Polanski – we open and close on the door latch. With the interesting exceptions of *Chinatown* and *The Ninth Gate* (1999), his every film from here on will bring us full circle, either closing in the very settings where their stories began or ending in places very nearly identical. The two men in *Two Men and a Wardrobe* (*Dwaj ludzie z szafą*, 1958) return, in the last shot, to the sea from which they emerged in the first. We meet the unhappy married couple in *Knife in the Water* (*Nóz w wodzie*, 1962) as they drive toward us on a country highway and take our leave of them as they park at a crossroads on the same route, headed the other way – their backs turned to us now, changed, we can imagine, by their adventure. Or have they changed? By bringing us in a circle, Polanski generously leaves open the question of character transformation, and with it, his film's meaning. *Rosemary's Baby* (1968) opens and closes on the gothic rooftops of New York's Dakota apartments, *The Pianist* with Wladyslaw Szpilman at his piano playing Chopin. It is left for us to say whether Szpilman or Rosemary have been altered by their many choices. Polanski never dictates, never preaches. Yet he so faithfully adheres to a principle of dramatic unity (derived from Aristotle's *Poetics*) that over time, such rhyming communicates a moral position. As vehemently as he renounces organized religion, Polanski places his faith in Creation, in living creative power. As nihilistic, or as demonically circular as many of his endings may be in terms of the hard fates meted out to his characters, the implication is always that, in the very act of giving our attention to a unified work of art, we are sharing with its maker in a ritual of hope.

His next short, *Teeth Smile* (*Usmiech zebiczny*, 1957) is a funny little two-minute exercise in which a dapper night-owl, headed for an evening out, is bewitched by a bare-breasted beauty he sights through a window while descending a flight of stairs. He stares for a long moment, lust filling his face. The next shot makes a closer study of this beauty's body. When a night-shirted neighbour pops open a nearby door to put out some bottles, the startled, embarrassed voyeur composes himself, and continues descending the stairs – only to pause when the neighbour has gone back inside. He then races back to the window, but now there is no naked female. A night-shirted man (the neighbour from before?) stands there instead, brushing his teeth and rolling his eyes in quietly berserk, foamy-mouthed ecstasy. Once again, the action ends where it began, on the stairs, but the interaction here is more intricate – there are 11 shots, in all. Each fresh angle significantly advances the narrative. Polanski relies entirely on the innate rhythmic pressures within a given shot, and cuts to the next strictly when there is a need for new information.

There is also one glimpse of genius. When the dandy voyeur is making his decision to race back for a second peek, he stretches out his hand like a sleepwalker and briefly touches his own shadow, which is now blackly immense on the wall

beside him. Actor Nikola Todorow (the cameraman who shot *The Bicycle*) moves through this swift, absent-minded gesture like a dancer floating through a turn, and Polanski calls no special attention to it – yet there it is, a graphic instant of psychological shift as valuable to the action as it is subtle.

His third exercise was supposed to be a documentary, but as Polanski would laugh years later, 'I had no vocation for documentaries.' So, he staged a prank that made certain he would have something interesting to film. He organized a dance on the Film School grounds, and on the sly arranged for a gang of local delinquents to crash the party. There was one technical hitch – they were too eager to oblige. 'I asked them to break up the dance about 12 o'clock,' he would recall, 'but the sons of bitches broke it up in half an hour.' Polanski was nearly expelled. His fellow students were much angrier with him than was the faculty, however, who viewed the raw footage with grudging admiration, and after a reprimand, permitted him to finish the film. *Break Up the Dance* (*Rozbijemy zabawe*, 1957) is thus a fascinating mongrel – a suspenseful, high-energy slice of life, ten minutes in length, that quickly turns into an action piece and by chance gives a quick glimpse of what a liberation jazz was for young Polish people in the Soviet era. The camerawork is elegant – from an over-the-shoulder shot of the host's hands, to a whip-pan which reveals the bullies. They sullenly stare in at the party from outside the mansion's leafy grounds, gripping the iron bars of the fence. When they decide to scale the fence *en masse*, they swarm it like prisoners making a break. Polanski films them from low angles evocative of exuberance and menace. The film begins at twilight, amid the hoisting of lanterns and a paper scarecrow, and ends at daybreak, contemplating the same objects, wrecked and torn, the scarecrow floating like a little dead man in the campus swimming pool.

Several in Polanski's circle later made great names for themselves. Boxer and poet Jerzy Skolimowski, who co-wrote *Knife in the Water*, would emerge as a superb director of such films as *Deep End* (1971) and *Moonlighting* (1982). Jerzy Kosinski, then studying photography, survived the holocaust because his cunning father moved their family east, virtually to the Russian front, where the Nazis were loath to go looking for Jews. He listened to Polanski's tales of a childhood on the run and later wove them into his most admired novel, *The Painted Bird* (1966). Krzystof Komeda was a medical doctor, who became a musician. By the time Polanski met him, he was Poland's leading jazz pianist and composer. Kris Malkiewicz was training as a cinematographer, and would later write the definitive textbook in English on the topic. Another classmate, Adam Holender, would photograph *Midnight Cowboy* (1969) for director John Schlesinger.

The West, particularly America, held a steady allure for each of these ambitious spirits. Now that Polanski was free within the curriculum to propose short films of an entirely original design, the West was where he cast his coldest eye. He had been born in Paris and his sister Annette now lived there, so he could obtain an exit visa, whereas most of his classmates could not. He managed a brief trip to France in 1957, visiting his sister and making a brief detour to the Cannes Film Festival. He was tempted to stay and seek political asylum. However, he realized the program at Lodz provided him with an excellent chance of making not just one but several good films in the coming year. That settled it. He returned home confident he could leverage a later escape on more suitable terms.

Stills from 'End of the Night' ('Koniec nocy', 1957)
In his 20s, Polanski was typecast as scrappy young toughs. Onstage, he has in recent years played Mozart in 'Amadeus', and Gregor Samsa in Kafka's 'Metamorphosis'.

Early Mastery
1958–1962

The 1958 World's Fair in Brussels announced an experimental film competition and Polanski decided he wanted to win. He even framed his proposal to the faculty in these terms. The film he outlined had been incubating in his head for a while: an absurdist allegory about two men who emerge from the sea bearing some ridiculously cumbersome object which causes them to be despised and rejected wherever they go. Polanski originally thought they should carry a grand piano, but feared this would be construed as a symbol of artistic talent, which was not what he wanted to say. Instead he needed a burden which would, on its surface, be completely meaningless, but could, in its puzzling neutrality, become infinitely suggestive. So, he afflicted his heroes with a bulky wardrobe cabinet.

There was also a strict artistic principle he hoped to apply. After viewing countless shorts projected in the mansion's upstairs ballroom, and after countless hours of arguing with his classmates while seated on the seventh step of the school stairwell, Polanski concluded that the best short films are those done entirely in pantomime. Music? Yes. Layered sound effects? Absolutely. Dialogue? Never. 'Shorts are either cartoons or documentaries, for me. When you use people in a short, if they talk you expect it's going to last for two hours. It's not natural, not proper to the form.'

Two Men and a Wardrobe (*Dwaj ludzie z szafą*, 1958) is thus no mere baby step in Polanski's filmography, but Opus #1 – his first work made for public consumption, and a prodigious debut. It also marks the first of his many fruitful collaborations with composer Komeda, whose lilting score sets just the right tones and counter-notes as the two heroes (Jakub Goldberg and Henryk Kluba) pop out of the sea carrying their comical load and commence their landward odyssey. Indeed, they seem to steer by Komeda's music (though it was added later). Polanski's direction and his composer's ability to communicate moods of isolation, joy, melancholy and stoic resolve are beautifully integrated. The men are at first joyful to be on land. They spruce themselves up in the wardrobe's big mirror, turn somersaults and wrestle like off-duty circus clowns. Polanski chose his players precisely for the cartoony vividness of their physiques, and their lack of acting experience. They never 'project' for the camera; they simply do for themselves, as if nobody is watching. They carry their wardrobe to town, but find they cannot board a bus, eat at a restaurant or check into a hotel. Even when they boldly rescue a pretty girl from a gang of bullies, she does not give them so much as a backward glance. The bullies on the other hand are delighted to have a pair of fresh victims upon whom they may freely administer a beating. In this, they are led by Polanski in a cameo appearance. (Years later, in *Chinatown*, he would intrude once again on his protagonist and do him even more harm.) After a few more misadventures, the two surrender, take up their wardrobe and, without complaint, carry it back into the sea. On their way to the water's edge, they carefully tiptoe through a wide horizon of little sandcastles that a small boy is busy manufacturing with his pail.

The film won a bronze medal at the World's Fair, launching Polanski. In terms of pure technique, he makes a significant advance that was also to become an abiding part of his storytelling vocabulary – most visibly in *Chinatown*. He subtly keeps the camera in constant motion, yet he never executes showy, complex masters. Rather, he devises simple, panning compositions which in one stroke reveal a wealth of information. When the two carry their cargo across a bridge, our gaze moves laterally, as if toward their destination, but in the process we come close upon a stranger who is picking another's pocket. Later still, tracking our wardrobe men as

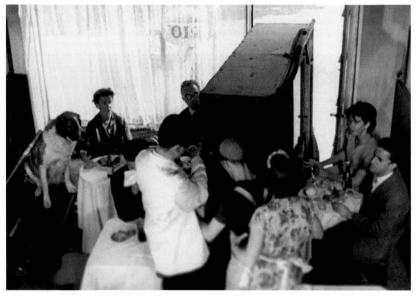

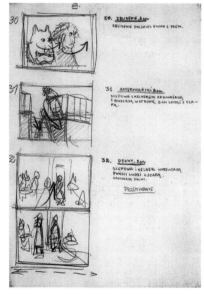

OPPOSITE
Still and storyboard from 'Two Men and a Wardrobe' (1958)
Polanski's boyhood love of cartoons blossomed into a skill for drafting storyboards, and a fondness for cartoonish live actors such as Henryk Klube and Jakub Goldberg. The second storyboard has a diagram showing the camera position for each shot.

PAGES 18/19
Photo of Roman Polanski
The Lodz school insisted Polanski train as a photographer before making films. This early experiment already communicates a world of the most intense alienation and comic zest.

ABOVE
Still and storyboard from 'Two Men and a Wardrobe' (1958)
Being ejected from a restaurant. Polanski drew 33 pages of storyboards, mapping compositions and movements within the frame, detailed down to that woman and her dog in panel two.

TOP
Still and storyboard from 'Two Men and a Wardrobe' (1958)
A slapstick battle is about to erupt, literally involving slaps with sticks pried from empty barrels. The 4th panel of the storyboard is the one realized in this photograph.

they move past an elegant façade framed by ancient trees, the foreground of the shot suddenly reveals a more ferocious crime; a man beating another to death. These ugly, common brutalities of human life heighten the angelic nature of the two wardrobe-bearers and their ever-hopeful progress, even as they wind their way back to oblivion. For however costly their burden, at least they are in motion, they are headed somewhere. Their persecutors are stuck.

Opus #2 is *The Lamp* (*Lampa*, 1959), an exquisite, dreamlike visit to a run-down toy shop. We can see the shop's elderly owner as the camera moves in from the street on a cold winter evening. Blink and you'll miss him, but Polanski is the first pedestrian to hurry by. A horse and carriage jingle past in the opposite direction. Komeda's music, and the shimmer of fairy-light inside the shop, gives the scene a jewel-box, storybook glow. Inside, close up, the toymaker is at work fitting a ceramic doll with eyes that blink. This interesting surgery has a slightly comical creepiness, given that the doll is so lovingly sculpted as to be lifelike. As the toymaker caps her with a little wig, then stretches to light his long-stemmed cigarette in the glass-chimneyed oil-lamp on his worktable, the shelves behind him reveal a world of countless such dolls. Tiny limbs, legless and armless torsos, row upon row of eyeless heads. The walls behind them are papered with newsprint, a century of forgotten headlines. As Polanski's eye tours these shadowy faces, they evoke cherubs and angels, as well as victims of the death camps. This ambiguity is delicate, but chilling. Then, a mini-flashback; workers' hands noisily rivet a new electrical lighting system into place. Their hammering sounds like gunfire, and the tiny transformer they leave on the shop's wall looks like a little voodoo face. (Its button-fuses look like bugging eyes, its meter like gritted teeth.) The toymaker ignores it. He closes for the night, extinguishing his oil lamp and boarding over the front window.

In the pitch dark after he exits, two mysterious events occur. Through the alchemy of Polanski's cutting and his careful, low-light compositions, the skull-like doll faces flicker with interior life. The soundtrack fills with other-worldly whispers, as if the toys are communicating in their keeper's absence. A second mysterious event follows; as these urgent voices reach their crescendo, the voodoo-faced fuse box suddenly explodes into flame. Fire climbs the shelves, ignites the paper walls, and then, by accelerating degrees, blackens and consumes the multitude of little beings. Did the dolls provoke this explosion, by way of an existential prison break? Or is Polanski mourning the devilish intrusion of electricity into a world of beauty that thrives best by firelight? Certainly you could never ask for a more poetic image of a child's world interrupted by a holocaust. The last shot of the film is a bravura repeat of the first, only moving away, now. As the blaze does its deadly work behind boarded-up windows, the dying shop itself becomes a lamp. The same pedestrians again hurry by; among them Polanski, but they are as oblivious to this wonder just over their shoulders as the ploughman in Breughel's painting *The Fall of Icarus* is to the miracle happening right behind him.

His diploma piece, *When Angels Fall* (*Gdy spadaja anioly*, 1959) is the longest, most ambitious and arguably the most heart-rending of all his shorts. Polanski had read in a newspaper about an elderly lavatory attendant who had experienced a mystical vision in her workplace, and was moved to wonder how such a person, who to his eyes led a life of unthinkable drudgery, could find her way to a passionate and even transcendent inner life. He found the elderly woman who plays the lead in a state home for the destitute. She was over 80 and had little idea what

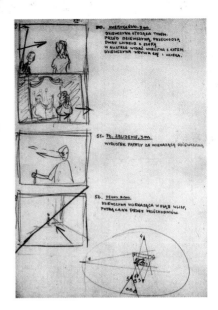

ABOVE
Still and storyboard from 'Two Men and a Wardrobe' (1958)
Panel 2 of the storyboard matches the photograph. A young tough hopes to frighten a beautiful girl with a dead cat, but she is warned by his skulking reflection in the wardrobe mirror.

OPPOSITE TOP
On the set of 'Two Men and a Wardrobe' (1958)
Roman Polanski, aged 24, leading the gang of hooligans who torment the two heroes.

OPPOSITE BOTTOM
Still from 'Two Men and a Wardrobe' (1958)
The two men wait for a tram. Polanski, in sunglasses at left, serves as an extra in addition to his role as a hoodlum. Budget constraints often forced him to make multiple use of himself, his cast and crew.

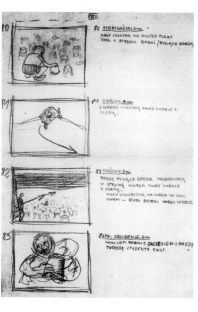

ABOVE
On the set of 'Two Men and a Wardrobe' (1958)
Polanski (right) in his suit and necktie shows his crewmen Andrzej Kostenko and Andrez Kijowski that, on 'his' set, he is all business.

LEFT
On the set of 'Two Men and a Wardrobe' (1958)
And, if your storyboards do not cover a needed camera-setup? Draw a line in the sand.

OPPOSITE TOP
Still from 'Two Men and a Wardrobe' (1958)
The two have a moment of respite beside their place of origin, the sea.

OPPOSITE BOTTOM
Still and storyboard from 'Two Men and a Wardrobe' (1958)
A winding return to the sea, meticulously planned on paper. The two traverse an image of human sweetness – the innocent (if slightly monstrous) industry of a child building sandcastles.

BELOW
Still from 'The Lamp' (1959)
Amid the flicker of light and shadow, one may
project either divine sweetness or demonic intent
upon the faces of these abandoned dolls.

OPPOSITE TOP
Still from 'When Angels Fall' (1959)
This woman had never acted before, yet the
camera drinks her face in. We are gazing in
anticipation at someone's inner world.

OPPOSITE BOTTOM LEFT
Still from 'When Angels Fall' (1959)
When young (played by Barbara Kwiatkowska),
this elderly heroine was carried in the arms of
"her" soldier (Andrzej Kondratiuk).

OPPOSITE BOTTOM RIGHT
On the set of 'When Angels Fall' (1959)
Kwiatkowska shyly tests the waters with her toe,
alongside her director and future husband,
Roman Polanski.

she was doing, but submitted meekly to Polanski's directions; her performance is marvellous. Kazimierz Wisniak, his production designer, created an elaborate, art deco-style lavatory on the film school's soundstage. Each of the ceramic urinals is crowned with rococo shells and has working pipes. Above all, there is a glass ceiling whose frosted squares fill the place with artfully created daylight and cast shadows of the drumming foot-traffic on the cleverly implied city sidewalk overhead. Polanski and Wisniak copied this latter detail from an existing lavatory in Kraków's medieval city centre. They also devised an enchantingly detailed model of Kraków itself, seen from above, which fills the film's opening and closing shots. This recreation is so effective that, at first glance, one might mistake it for the actual cityscape. Then, as one's eyes adjust and discover the artifice, Krzystof Komeda's music, with its traces of accordion and tolling bells, gives a dreamy sense of a city made of gingerbread. We are in any case gazing in anticipation at someone's inner world. This sets the stage for magic to happen, and helps lighten the film's first few minutes, as the elderly crone makes her way through the actual Kraków (beauty caked with soot and rubble) to the subterranean lavatory where she spends her dingy days. Gradually, the incessant tapping of water drops and the drumming of feet on the sidewalk above softly evoke the swaggering, martial beat of singing soldiers, long ago. And on this note the film, which up to now had been in black & white, bursts into full colour. A soldier (whom we may assume to be 'her' soldier) appears in solitude along a tree-plumed horizon, and is shortly joined by his fellows.

This is Polanski's first work in colour, and his first foray into recreating a historical period. His work here is as meticulous as it would ever be (and that is saying something), legibly tracing the late glory of the Austro-Hungarian Empire, circa 1895, to the First World War of 1914. His storytelling methods are of necessity elliptical, as he leaps decades in a single cut, without dialogue. He concentrates as much information as he can into each single composition. As she ignores the visitors to the washroom (pedestrians, drunks and men seeking sex) the woman stares up at the glass squares in the ceiling, which dissolve to Technicolor and become blossoms floating in a stream. Our heroine, radiantly young and breathtakingly beautiful, is carried over the water by 'her' soldier, who lovingly dips down so she can scoop these blossoms into an impromptu bouquet. Without a cut, the soldier plants her onshore, hugs her from the legs up and spins her out of frame. When they return (again, no cuts), they are much further along in their lovemaking. They plump into the soft grass; in his ardour the soldier's patent-leather hat topples into the water and is carried away by the current. Here, Polanski cuts, and on the fade up, the young woman is now tending to a small baby while her angry father taps at the window from the outside and mutely browbeats her for not attending to her other chores. The empty rows of farmland behind him stretch backward in the frame to the vanishing point, a subtle indication that she has been abandoned.

Polanski thus manages to fit a mini-epic into these twenty minutes. The baby grows to manhood, is dragged off to join the army, coldly ignores his mother when she moves to the city to be near him and tries to offer him a bundle of food. Polanski plays the old woman in middle age, and quite well. We are shown what she imagines to be her boy's adventures on the battlefield and his lonely death. Finally, as darkness falls in the lavatory, the glass in the ceiling shatters and her lost son descends, standing on the tiles as a white-winged, warmly smiling angel. Is this the moment of her death? Possibly, for we retreat above the skylight and, to a surge of Komeda's music, contemplate the toy-like rooftops again, as heavenly snow falls.

ABOVE
On the set of 'When Angels Fall' (1959)
Polanski and actor Andrzej Kondratiuk stage the
death of the elderly woman's lost son under a
tree which, in a dreamy but fitting touch, bears
fruit in wintertime.

RIGHT
On the set of 'When Angels Fall' (1959)
With cameraman Henryk Kucharski (left),
Polanski made the most of the Lodz school's
professional-grade soundstages in recreating a
Kraków public lavatory.

The striking beauty who played this woman when young was actress Barbara Kwiatkowska, later known in the West as Barbara Lass. She was also the first Mrs Roman Polanski. They met shortly after he had won the prize at Brussels for *Two Men and a Wardrobe*. She got noticed abroad after starring in *Eva Wants to Sleep* (*Ewa chce spac*, 1958), and was being written about as "the Polish Bardot". What is more evident now is that her particular beauty (ripe figure, lush mouth, heavy-lidded, feline eyes) foretells Polanski's attractions to both Sharon Tate and Nastassja Kinski. There is a moment in *When Angels Fall*, when she stands at her window, enraptured, that could serve across the intervening twenty years as a coming attraction for *Tess* (1979). When Lass was invited to Paris to star in a film, Polanski went with her, sweet-talking the Polish ambassador there into giving himself and Lass a pair of consular passports – coveted documents which allowed them both to travel freely. He also wasted no time in setting up French financing for another film.

The Fat and the Lean (*Le gros et le maigre*, *Gruby i chudy*, 1961) is a revealing fable of where Polanski felt himself to be at this point in his life. His anger at the Soviet system boils very close to its surface, though he takes care at every step to make the most universal statement he can. The setting is a run-down chateau in the French countryside. Polanski plays "The Lean", a human performing-pet who drums, plays flute, dances, cooks and otherwise waits hand and foot on "The Fat" (Andrzej Katelbach), a porky tyrant enthroned in an easy chair. Lean, who can see the Eiffel Tower in the misty distance from his kitchen window, makes several escape attempts. At first, Fat wins him back with bribery – he gives him a pet goat. When Lean makes a second run for it (bewitched as ever by that view of Paris in the distance), Fat catches him again – only this time he chains him to the goat. Now Lean must attempt to dance, entertain, make meals and music with a ridiculous burden cinched to his ankle – the most politically charged metaphor in the film. Fat is such a palpable old Bolshevik, down to his Khrushchev buzz-cut and the military medal in his lapel, that we are inescapably led to think of Soviet-style *apparatchiks* and how they would hobble workers and artists alike by making absurd, counterproductive demands. Yet Polanski makes this power struggle universal by keeping it funny. (As a comic film actor, he has a basic gift in common with his heroes Charlie Chaplin and Buster Keaton, which is that when he is in motion, you cannot take your eyes off him.) Moreover, structurally, he repeatedly demonstrates that his two creatures are fatally interdependent. When Lean makes a third and final attempt to flee, goat and all, toward the tower in the distance, Fat gives chase and, after their most physical shoving match, relents, cutting the goat free. Lean grovels for joy and kisses his master's feet. In the next fade up we discover he has been freshly bribed with a brand-new, Western-style drum kit, and has resumed his chores with high-stepping zest. Yet something has changed. While Fat sleeps, Lean quietly plants tulips in the grass all around them both, content to contemplate their beauty with the Eiffel Tower at his back.

The implication is that Lean is no longer a slave. He has developed an inner life his tormentor cannot see. For Polanski, with his own eye on the Eiffel Tower, this touching resolution must have served as a 'note to self', inscribed to strengthen his spirits if his luck reversed and he were to wind up stuck behind the Iron Curtain. It is, in any event, a heartfelt salute to the bravery and ingenuity of anyone who can hold onto their inner truth against great odds. This remains true whether the nearest bully is a Communist or a capitalist, but Polanski clearly felt it applied most painfully to those gentle and creative friends he foresaw himself leaving behind.

Still from 'When Angels Fall' (1959)
Barbara Kwiatkowska in a pose that foretells moments in 'The Fearless Vampire Killers' and 'Tess'. Waiting, watching and isolation are poten dramatic attitudes in Polanski's films.

ABOVE
Still from 'The Fat and the Lean' (1961)
Polanski, proving himself an agile silent comedian as "The Lean", slaves and fiddles at the behest of "The Fat" (Andrzej Katelbach).

RIGHT
Still from 'The Fat and the Lean' (1961)
A true Soviet-style bully, Fat corners Lean into his service with bribes (a pet goat) and inhuman punishments (chaining him to the goat).

Still from 'The Fat and the Lean' (1961)
Lean dreams of escape to Paris (note the Eiffel Tower behind him), but the tulips with which he surrounds himself represent his inner freedom.

LEFT
Still from 'The Fat and the Lean' (1961)
From his early teens onward, Polanski dreamt of escaping to the west. This film is his most complete expression of that dream.

ABOVE
Still from 'Mammals' (1962)
"Some faces cry out to be put on film," Polanski has written. It helps that nature also made Michal Zolnierkiewicz so monumentally tall, with such long comic stork-like limbs.

RIGHT
Still from 'Mammals' (1962)
Samuel Beckett admired Polanski's films, but refused to let him adapt 'Waiting for Godot'. So? As Oscar Wilde put it: 'Mediocrity borrows, Genius steals.'

BELOW
On the set of 'Mammals' (1962)
Polanski's friend, financier and, in this case, deputy cinematographer Wojtek Frykowski rides in the 'Lord & Master' position to get the best angle on the panting Zolnierkiewicz.

Perhaps he judged *The Fat and the Lean* to have too political an underbelly, for he quickly turned around and reworked the 'Master and Man' theme into a short script he called *Mammals*. Here, the tone would be far more freewheeling and absurdist. When he and Lass returned to Poland in late 1961, Polanski submitted the script to the State production unit that supervised shorts. They turned it down. His long-time friend Gene Gutowski offered to put up half the money – there being no law in Poland at that time against private film production. There was of course a very strict law (and this is an exquisite Soviet paradox) forbidding private ownership of film equipment. Polanski manoeuvred around this by securing the loan of a camera and other essentials from his old schoolmates in Lodz. With the help of some additional cash from another pal, Wojtek Frykowski, Polanski and his crew filmed for a week or so in Zakopane, high in the snow country of the Tatras mountains.

Mammals (*Ssaki*, 1962) smoothly fulfils Polanski's plans for it, and rounds out his career as a short film-maker on a delightful, valedictory note. The presence of Henryk Kluba, one of the actors in *Two Men and a Wardrobe*, lends a note of conscious symmetry – though where he was the taller and gawkier of the two in the earlier film, here he is the squat and agile one by contrast with his gigantic co-star Michal Zolnierkiewicz. As in *The Fat and the Lean,* there is a power struggle – in this case, a slapstick battle over who will be first among equals. The heroes are two Samuel Beckett-like stick figures who argue amid an infinitely snowy landscape about whose turn it is to ride the toy sled they share. Only one may ride at a time – the other has to don a harness and pull. So they manipulate each other in a series of sight-gags, engaging in trickery, feigning injury, even feigning invisibility when one wraps himself head-to-toe in white bandages. 'As in cartoons,' wrote Polanski, 'props appear on demand.' Whereas *Two Men and a Wardrobe* was allegorical and surreal, in the manner of Luis Buñuel's *L'Âge d'or* (1930), and whereas *The Fat and the Lean* recalls Chaplin with its built-in bonds of sympathy for the Pan-like charm of Polanski's Lean, *Mammals* lands us squarely in Keaton territory. This is true not only in its cartoony inventiveness (all those useful items coming so dreamily to hand), but in its refusal to solicit emotional sympathy for one character over the

other. There is also its punchline: while our two heroes bicker at their most extreme, a third party (Wojtek Frykowski, devouring sausages) slips into the picture and steals their sled.

Buñuel, Chaplin, Keaton… by the time he was ready to make features, Polanski had mastered the whole palette of classic silent cinema. And he had found his own style: flexible, translucent, equal to every note and occasion. When there needs to be a close-up, there is a close-up, elegant and absolute. Two-shots, masters and travelling shots all braid together with seamless ease. At age 28, Polanski directs as he will at 70, leading us to concentrate on content. Yet if we care to study his methods (hitting the freeze-frame button on an average of every five seconds) it is clear he has privately concentrated the largest share of his creative energies on excellence of form, all with the goal of making form disappear and what we experience more meaningful.

'A couple on a small yacht take aboard a passenger who disappears under mysterious circumstances.' Such was the premise Polanski worked up in 1959 (after finishing *When Angels Fall*) with his pal Jakub Goldberg. He set to work with Jerzy Skolimowski at transforming it into a feature-length screenplay. With his training as a poet, Skolimowski was ideal for helping Polanski keep words to a minimum. He also shared his passion for dramatic unity, and proposed they restrict the action of the story to a 24-hour period. They cooped themselves up for five nights straight, acted out the roles as they composed and emerged with a taut, intimate, action-driven thriller they called *Knife in the Water*. 'Lack of social commitment' was the verdict from the Polish Ministry of Culture, which denied Polanski funding. Polanski translated the script into French and tried unsuccessfully to make it there during the year he was in Paris. Upon finishing *Mammals* in early 1962, he added a few lines of 'socially conscious' dialogue (though true to his own style he laced these into the seduction scene) and resubmitted the script. This time it was approved.

Polanski led a crew to Poland's spectacular Mazury lake district. Shooting on water was a nightmare – boats kept shifting position, shadows radically slanted in accordance, and skies either filled too quickly with clouds or emptied twice as fast. It

ABOVE
Still from 'Mammals' (1962)
Henryk Kluba, the taller, freakier clown in 'Two Men and a Wardrobe', here looks (despite the extremity of his costume) comparatively diminutive and ordinary.

LEFT
Still from 'Mammals' (1962)
The film shows the characters battle for a place on the sled.

BELOW
On the set of 'Mammals' (1962)
Riding in style, actor Henryk Kluba and director Polanski.

was easy for him to foresee that at the editing table, months later, it would be hell to find any two shots that matched in continuity, so he drove his crew to work all the harder. There were also difficulties with the actors. Polanski cast an experienced professional, Leon Niemczyk, as the macho husband, and a drama student, Zygmunt Malanowicz, as the fallen-angelic hitch-hiker. For the wife, he found a non-professional, Jolanta Umecka, a beauty he noticed as she emerged dripping from a local swimming pool. Such variants in talent created a myriad of problems akin to the drift of the boats. To get a proper look of surprise out of Umecka at one point, Polanski resorted to firing a flare-gun off camera, and he ended up dubbing his own voice in place of Malanowicz on the soundtrack, to take full charge of his performance. "But it's the result that matters," as he says, and these difficulties are nowhere in evidence in the finished film. If anything, Polanski reversed these negatives to completely positive effect. If Niemczyk is the most accomplished performer of the three, it lends extra force to the husband's 'role' as instigator of the film's conflicts. If the actress is inert in life, in the context of the drama she seems sphinx-like, ambiguous, the keeper of the film's secrets. The youth may well be, as Polanski once said in an interview, "Just a device. The real story is between the husband and wife," yet as a character, he shows up wreathed in layers of ambiguity that are personal to him.

The youth nearly causes a car crash when he first appears on the misty roadway. The husband has to swerve and hit the brakes. The young man is strangely unapologetic. The husband's curses roll off him. The wife, watching from her passenger seat, is amused, which irks the husband. Then, moments later, shifting his tack, he invites the youth to ride with them. The couple have stolen a day to go sailing. They need to be back in the city by morning. The young man drifts with them, either spurred by the husband's challenges to his pride or attracted to the wife, who becomes more radiantly sensual as the trio set sail. The day is driven by physical contests, large and small. The husband is an able sailor, the youth inept, unable even to swim, he says. Yet he scales the mast with the ease of a monkey, and

ABOVE
On the set of 'Mammals' (1962)
Working quickly, without sound, Polanski's assistant Andrzej Kostenko simply slates the shot for scene number and take.

RIGHT
On the set of 'Mammals' (1962)
"That's a wrap." Polanski relaxes with his merry cast and crew: Henryk Kluba, Andrzej Kostenko, Michal Zolnierkiewicz and cameraman Andrzej Kondratiuk.

proves dexterous with a knife. He can rapidly tap the sharp blade to and fro between his fingers; a dangerous trick he makes look easy. When a sudden rainstorm moves them below deck, the husband in turn shows himself to be a natural at throwing the knife, striking a target-board across the room with snakebite accuracy. Polanski and cinematographer Jerzy Lipman mint superb, silvery images when the action is outdoors. A brief sequence when the men must pull the boat through a thicket of deep grass, testing each other as they trudge, is graphically dazzling. So too are those moments when the wife is shown in her enigmatic isolation, her lazy prone figure aligned with the gliding horizon, a middle-class Cleopatra feeling her power. When the action moves down into the hold, the pictorial elegance turns psychological in value. The youth tries to avert his eyes as the wife towels off and dons a bathrobe, naked for a second. The husband watches him, vaguely amused and predatory in one fiery glance.

In a 1972 television interview, film critic Charles Champlin teasingly accused Polanski of "Christian symbolism" in his visual treatment of the youth. Polanski, showing his gift for acting, gasped "What do you mean????" Champlin was referring to the indelible image of the young man, spreading his arms wide, feet crossed, as he lies on the yacht's needle-like prow. Seen from high above, his head conveniently haloed by a coiled rope, he recalls Christ on the cross. "An accident," laughed

ABOVE
On the set of 'Knife in the Water' (1962)
A 'hands on' director from head to toe, Polanski
perches precariously aboard the warring
couple's Mercedes, alongside cameraman Jerzy
Lipman.

RIGHT
On the set of 'Knife in the Water' (1962)
Polanski chose a Mercedes because this was
the sort of car a ranking member of the party
would drive.

Polanski. "The rope, you see, was simply there to cushion his head because he lacked a pillow. And he spreads his arms so, because, you know, he wants a better suntan." Yet the image is there, and nothing is accidental with Polanski. Certainly, the young man is no Christ-figure in any traditional sense; judged by his actions, he is more of a tempter, a malevolent angel, a serpent in the garden. As the film moves to its climax, he even enacts a death and resurrection. He and the husband fight. The youth topples overboard and does not resurface. (In reality, he is clinging to a buoy just out of the couple's sight.) This is a cruel joke on the husband, who is wracked with guilt that his bullying may have cost the young man his life, but it is also a seductive gesture toward the wife. When the husband leaves the boat, swimming desperately for shore in search of his victim, the youth slips back on board, startles the wife (cue flare gun) and makes love to her. That he is still alive after this misadventure, and slips ashore undetected, remains a little secret between himself and the wife. She now has something to hold over her husband, whom she sees shivering on the dock as she brings the boat in alone. The husband has turned his guilt into an erotic fascination that he has actually proved himself to be hard and lethal in front of his woman. This adds a note of sexy tension to their bickering as they sit at the film's final crossroads.

"You can have no idea how liberating an experience *Knife in the Water* was for the rest of us in Polish cinema when it first came out," Andrzej Wajda told Lawrence Weschler of *The New Yorker*, four decades later in 1994. "For the first time since the war, here was a film that didn't have anything to do with the war... [Roman] was all about starting afresh ... I'm sure that in part accounted for its breakthrough success abroad – the critics' prize at the Venice festival, the cover of *Time*, the Oscar nomination." Yet despite such remarkably global adulation, the film received a whipping in the Polish State press. Even Poland's ruler, Wladyslaw Gomulka, announced the film was "Neither typical of nor relevant to Poland as a whole".

Polanski decided not to wait for any further thunderbolts from on high. He packed his car and, brandishing his still-valid passport, drove West. That *Knife in the Water* had won such attention in America, especially the cover of *Time* (a startling coup, even in retrospect) was proof that Polanski's fortunes as an international director were his to claim. There were still many practical obstacles (language, money) but he had faced down tougher ones.

"Roman was an insatiable presence on the set back then. Voraciously interested in everything technical. Lighting, film stock, camera optics – with no interest whatever, on the other hand, with the sorts of thematic concerns that obsessed the rest of us, like politics, Poland's place in the world, and, especially, our recent national past. He saw everything in front of him and nothing behind, his eyes firmly fixed on a future he already seemed to be hurtling toward at maximum speed. And for him, that future was out there, in the world, and particularly in Hollywood, which he equated with the world standard in cinema. Even then. And that was absolutely unique among us."

Andrzej Wajda

Still from 'Knife in the Water' (1962)
After pressure from the press the producers ordered Polanski to reshoot the car's exteriors, downgrading it from a bourgeois Mercedes to a people's Peugeot. Here affluent Andrzej (Leon Niemczyk) baits and is baited by the unnamed rebel drifter (Zygmunt Malanowicz).

ABOVE
Still from 'Knife in the Water' (1962)
Polanski discovered sailing while a student. He
was thrilled by the skill involved, and the
freedom of it. Krystyna (Jolanta Umecka) and
Andrzej look so at home on the water that it is
small wonder Western audiences so freely
embraced the film.

RIGHT
On the set of 'Knife in the Water' (1962)
Special effects create misty rain. Filming on
water caused so many technical problems that
Polanski would film close to shore as often as a
particular set of shots permitted.

ABOVE
On the set of 'Knife in the Water' (1962)
Harold Lloyd or the Marx Brothers were at home in such predicaments. For Polanski and his cast and crew, it was a daily hurdle.

LEFT
On the set of 'Knife in the Water' (1962)
Cameraman Jerzy Lipman braves autumn-cold water to get a more elegant low angle asked for by Polanski (centre).

OPPOSITE TOP
Still from 'Knife in the Water' (1962)
A macho competition between men of two generations, into which one can read an allegory of the struggle for control of a country.

OPPOSITE BOTTOM LEFT
Still from 'Knife in the Water' (1962)
Tests of dexterity with a knife then give way to a contest of strength, as the two males tow the boat through deep grass.

OPPOSITE BOTTOM RIGHT
Still from 'Knife in the Water' (1962)
This, in turn, swells into a battle of wills over a woman. Andrzej is not merely clever with a knife, but deadly.

ABOVE
Still from 'Knife in the Water' (1962)
The rivalry between husband and drifter finally erupts into a fistfight in which the younger man topples overboard, and appears to drown.

RIGHT
On the set of 'Knife in the Water' (1962)
Interiors were filmed later on a Warsaw soundstage. Polanski (centre, looking fragile) fractured his skull in a car wreck, but discharged himself from the hospital against doctor's orders to finish the film.

PAGES 42 & 43
On the set of 'Knife in the Water' (1962)
Polanski and cameraman Lipman in harnesses. Athletic demands were made of the whole cast and crew, but it is clear most relished the challenges.

OPPOSITE TOP
Still from 'Knife in the Water' (1962)
He is risen. With the husband gone in search of
him, the young man returns to seduce the wife.

OPPOSITE BOTTOM LEFT
Still from 'Knife in the Water' (1962)
The seduction. Polanski and co-writer Jerzy
Skolimowski cleverly used the build-up to this
clinch to get rid of whatever 'social realist'
dialogue the authorities required.

OPPOSITE BOTTOM RIGHT
On the set of 'Knife in the Water' (1962)
Note the plank under Jolanta Umecka, to better
support her in her kisses with Zygmunt
Malanowicz. It will not be seen in the close-ups.
Polanski hovers over the actors, giving direction.
The film was shot silent and the Polanski used
his own voice for the young man.

ABOVE
Still from 'Knife in the Water' (1962)
The wife knows the youth is alive, but is not
telling. The husband torments himself over the
ambiguity, but these dynamics only add fresh
spice to their marriage as they drive away.

A Charmed Life
1963–1969

ROMAN POLA

What is fascinating about *Repulsion* (1965), *Cul-de-Sac* (1966), *The Fearless Vampire Killers* (1967) and *Rosemary's Baby* (1968), especially when considered in relation to the hardships of Polanski's childhood, is that he refused to be mired in all that past suffering. His innate optimism led him to be playful about darkness and dread, to seek catharsis in worlds of fantasy. It is also significant that he should excel at creating such fascinating, complex women at the centre of his films. For all his macho bluster in interviews of the period, it is clear such posturing was the suit of armour which allowed everything that was most archetypically female in Polanski (his vulnerability, his emotional awareness, his unpredictability and raw creative power) to remain safely hidden yet free to emerge in the work. Perhaps these women are a mythic legacy of his mother; perhaps they are an imaginative encryption of himself as a child. Polanski has never ever been interested in looking back for its own sake. (As close to his own life as *The Pianist* is in theme and sense-memory, it makes sense that, even pushing 70, he could only revisit such terrors by going back disguised as an adult.) He is an artist on whom no experience is lost, yet the past only matters to him in terms of practical use. His early childhood, spent exploring the immensities of an apartment-house stairwell, or his later moves through the ghetto and into hiding, held no charm for him – but they became extremely useful when tracing the disintegration of a fictional young London woman whose loneliness and fear are killing her sanity.

Repulsion (1965) was conceived as a strictly commercial idea. Polanski met writer Gérard Brach at a Paris cocktail party shortly after leaving Poland and a lifelong creative partnership was sparked on the spot. They quickly wrote an absurdist thriller they were enthused about, later called *Cul-de-Sac*, but could not get it produced. "Too original", was the death sentence. So they coldly assessed the market and rebounded with *Repulsion*, a piece superficially in the mould of Alfred Hitchcock's *Psycho* (1960): a one-word title, and a dreamy blonde in jeopardy. They sold it right away to The Compton Film Group. They designed it to work superficially as a blood-curdling horror movie. "Anything more sophisticated would have scared [Compton] off," Polanski knew. But they made it interesting for themselves by using peculiar people and situations they had observed in life. Carol, the doe-eyed manicurist who goes violently mad when her sister leaves on holiday, was based on a beauty they both knew. Everyone when alone sooner or later experiences the sense that someone is watching, or has heard that late-night creak in the floorboards that heralds (false alarm) a possible intruder. Polanski amplifies such everyday chills with expressionist zest. The walls, for Carol, not only 'have ears', as the saying goes in English, they have hands too, all of which are reaching out to cop a feel as she loses her last contact with reality and pinballs down the empty hallways in her sister's flat.

The hypnotic beauty of Catherine Deneuve (then a newcomer) justifies Carol's paranoia (every male in sight is indeed bidding for her sexual attentions), and misleads her few friends and relations into presuming that she is not only normal (despite foggy social skills) but content. Her spiral feels all the more tragic because her inward affliction is so at odds with her outer gifts. There is nothing logically inevitable about the way she falls apart. Instead she seems to be in the forceful grip of a malign fate, and from this Polanski and Brach wring a classical wealth of pity and terror. The no less Greek awe they provoke is a by-product of stylish unities; the first and last shots of the film are extreme close-ups of Carol's right eye. We either draw back from her pupil under the opening credits, as if from the black

ABOVE
Still from 'River of Diamonds' (1964)
Polanski contributed this lively half-hour chapter to an otherwise failed 'omnibus' film called 'The Beautiful Swindlers', and cast Nicole Karen (right) for her aura of amoral charm.

PAGES 46/47
On the set of 'The Fearless Vampire Killers' (1967)
Polanski inspects his fairytale vampire castle. Originally all the castle footage was to be shot on location in Austria, but on the eve of the shoot all the snow melted, so an expensive castle set was built and the snow scenes were shot in Italy.

Still from 'Repulsion' (1965)
Outwardly, Carol (Catherine Deneuve) has
beauty and a silent vulnerability, which everyone
around her mistakes for shyness, even
sweetness. This is her deadly illness in subtle
disguise. The only clues to her inner world,
before we cross over, come through distorted
reflections – either in mirrors, or in this teapot.

depths of outermost space, or, in the closing moment, are guided to a photo of
Carol as a young girl, where it is clear the madness which will someday consume
her is already asserting itself, in her transfixed stare. Again we move in on her right
eye and back into oblivion. Polanski, an admirer of Stanley Kubrick's *Dr Strangelove*
(1964), hired its cinematographer, Gilbert Taylor, and the images they coin as Carol
drifts absently through her workday have metaphoric power. Her first manicure
client, lying under a sheet and white facial mudpack, recalls a mummified corpse.
Her withered fingers, clasped by young Carol's, evoke death in life and the fleeting
nature of beauty. Polanski conjures these not out of symbolism, but to communicate
how the world looks to Carol. He also follows her on her walks through downtown
London, often in complex masters without cuts. We seldom dwell on any passing
detail, apart from the advances of a road-worker. Instead, we spend much of our
time staring straight at the enigmatic back of Carol's head. A sense of dislocation
thus shadows her every step. Chico Hamilton's super-percussive jazz score (Komeda
having been unavailable) hammers this home energetically.

Tragedy and horror collide when a suitor (John Fraser) bursts in on Carol after
she has withdrawn from the world for over a week. Alone of all the other characters
in the film, he seems to truly love her. At the very least, he grasps what we in the
audience know, which is that she is not only unbalanced but close to a lethal cliff

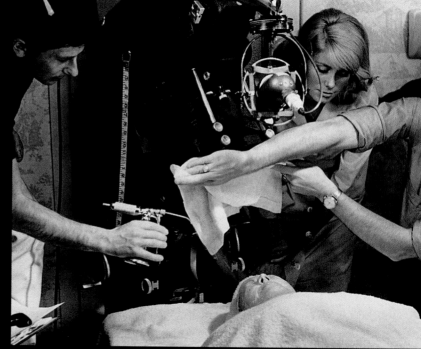

ABOVE
On the set of 'Repulsion' (1965)
Polanski tests the needle-touch of an aerosol gun against his own cheek.

TOP RIGHT
On the set of 'Repulsion' (1965)
True to his usual hands-on approach, Polanski sprays one of Carol's mummy-like clients at the salon. An assistant protects the camera lens with a swatch of cloth.

RIGHT
On the set of 'Repulsion' (1965)
Polanski (in mirror) works with Deneuve, assessing how to best portray Carol's illness. Her first instinct is to show she is in pain, but this proves too violent for the scene. They decide instead that Carol 'sees dirty things' and keeps brushing them away.

ABOVE
Still from 'Repulsion' (1965)
The full extent of Carol's illness is revealed only

ABOVE
On the set of 'Repulsion' (1965)
Polanski, behind Deneuve, accompanies her on
a walk-through. Carol only glimpses the
workman (Mike Pratt, right) as she walks home,
but night after night she will dream he rapes her.

RIGHT
On the set of 'Repulsion' (1965)
Working out camera angles. Although Polanski
pre-plans meticulously, he also remains
completely flexible, allowing the actors' choices
and the environment to influence him.

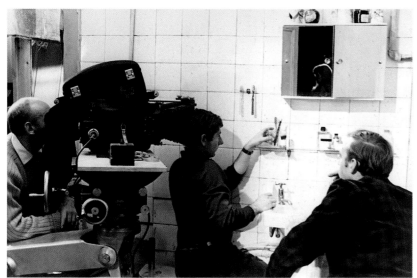

ABOVE
Still from 'Repulsion' (1965)
Carol is excitedly repulsed by Michael (Ian Hendry), her sister's lover. After he takes the sister on holiday, Carol uses his straight razor to murder every other intruder into her home.

LEFT
On the set of 'Repulsion' (1965)
Polanski adjusts the straight razor with his usual precision. He and cinematographer Gilbert Taylor worked hard to give the blade-edge just the right shine. In the end, they sheathed it in a strip of foil.

Still from 'Repulsion' (1965)
Colin (John Fraser) is the only compassionate man who pursues Carol, and who offers help when he sees she is breaking down. He is her first murder victim.

edge. He genuinely wants to help. When his back is turned, she bashes in his skull with a candlestick. His eyes are wide open in death, sad at this last surprise. As she slips him into a tub full of water, blood floats blackly from his mouth in a thick curling scarf; a perfectly horrid detail. She later kills her landlord and stacks him behind a sofa. When she is found by her returning sister, the neighbours are brought running from throughout the building in a nightmarish frenzy. Their staring faces, standing in for ours, hold a morbidly funny mirror (à la Hitchcock) to everybody's tendencies to be a voyeur.

Carol has shunned her sister's boyfriend Michael (Ian Hendry), but it is he who gently carries her away from staring eyes, her forbidden Prince Charming. From this moment of stolen peace, Polanski's camera floats backward and descends, without a cut, to the photo which reveals the nascently mad Carol, with her family long ago. In 1968, Joseph Gelmis asked if this final image is meant to imply that Carol was a victim of sexual molestation. (This is certainly the interpretation that springs to mind in the 21st century, when child abuse is so widely discussed.) Polanski answered no. "I just wanted to show that there was something wrong with the girl even then."

Still from 'Repulsion' (1965)
Note that dish of skinned rabbit, rotting in front
of the disintegrating Carol. Polanski had left it in
a dead refrigerator for weeks. The crew was
grateful for neither the stench nor the flies, but it
provides an unforgettably vivid marker for Carol's
tragic progress.

And much as he has been delighted that psychiatrists find his portrait of her
disintegration so well-realised, Polanski has no desire to embroider Carol's back-
story. His resistance is artistic. "The whole showmanship is *not* to answer every
question."

Cul-de-Sac (1966) is a pioneering fulfilment of this principle. When *Repulsion*
won a Silver Bear at the 1965 Berlin Film Festival, The Compton Group were
bowled over. They had never made a prestige picture before. Now they were
much more receptive when Polanski resubmitted the 'too original' comedy they
had previously brushed aside. Polanski and Brach wanted *Cul-de-Sac* to gratify
every mad wish and/or farcical impulse that they had always wanted to see in
a film. Both were under the spell of Samuel Beckett and Harold Pinter – Polanski
had once approached Beckett about the film rights to *Waiting for Godot*. One
of the working titles for *Cul-de-Sac* was even a direct homage: *When Katelbach
Comes*.

The setting is Holy Island, a remote British peninsula. Twice a day, coastal tides
erase the highway and turn it into an island. George (Donald Pleasance) has moved

LEFT
Still from 'Repulsion' (1965)
After our minds, it is our hands which set us apart from all other creatures. Polanski films them in concert. Carol's landlord (Patrick Wymark) frames her face with his hands, as rape enters his mind.

BOTTOM LEFT
On the set of 'Repulsion' (1965)
And hands become the foolish bully's futile line of defence when Carol responds to his advances with a straight razor.

BELOW
Still from 'Repulsion' (1965)
Note to Self – Carol writes a torrent of unknown words on her looking glass. Throughout the film, her hands are in motion.

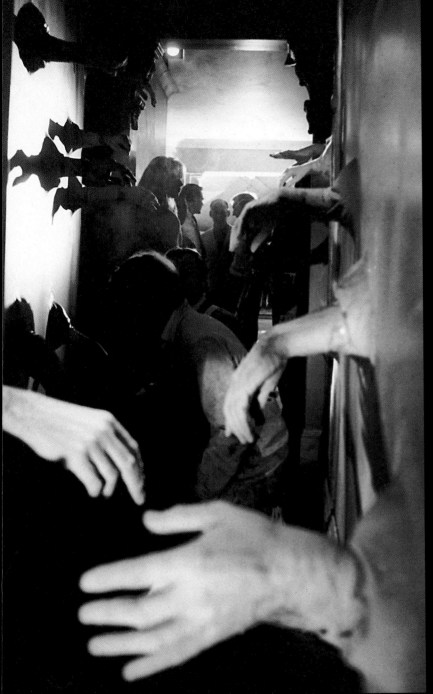

ABOVE
On the set of 'Repulsion' (1965)
Her universe fills with grasping hands. The apartment walls were made to widen or narrow with Carol's inflamed mental states.

ABOVE RIGHT
Still from 'Repulsion' (1965)
Carol's collapse lands her in the tender clasp of the dreaded Michael. When he returns with her sister and lifts her away from prying eyes, Carol does not resist.

PAGE 58 TOP
Still from 'Cul-de-Sac' (1966)
Françoise Dorléac, Catherine Deneuve's sister, plays the female lead in Polanski's next film. Her Teresa is a confident man-eater, here catching neighbour Christopher (Iain Quarrier) when they should be catching shrimp.

PAGE 58 BOTTOM
On the set of 'Cul-de-Sac' (1966)
Filming naked in the dunes despite temperatures ranging from cool to freezing.

PAGE 59 TOP
Still from 'Cul-de-Sac' (1966)
Teresa dominates husband George (Donald Pleasance) with a kinky sense of mischief. This scene was based on Polanski observing his wife Barbara impulsively putting make-up on producer Pierre Roustang in 1960.

PAGE 59 BOTTOM
On the set of 'Cul-de-Sac' (1966)
Polanski, Gilbert Taylor and Pleasance, who said that George was a man of "abnormal normality".

On the set of 'Cul-de-Sac' (1966)
While filming at high tide on the now submerged causeway to Holy Island, one of the production's jeeps is swallowed by the icy waves. Dorléac and Pleasance cling to a generator truck for warmth.

into the medieval castle on this isle with his beautiful but younger, friskier bride Teresa (Françoise Dorléac, elder sister of Catherine Deneuve). Their bubble of imagined tranquillity is rudely punctured when a fugitive American gangster named Dicky (the gravel-voiced Lionel Stander) staggers onto the island at low tide. He holds the couple hostage overnight as he waits for his boss, Mr Katelbach, to send a car or rescue plane. While he waits the three act out a psychological tug of war that is by turns erotic, humiliating and vicious. We can guess that Mr Katelbach, like Godot before him, will never quite come. As the first day stretches into two, other travellers happen onto the island (among them a young Jacqueline Bisset) and complicate matters still further.

Pinter's rule of threes is soundly enforced: put two people in a room and when things are about to boil over bring in a third. So too is Beckett's love of bare horizons and rhyming enigmas. The film's opening shot stares straight down the sand-swept causeway toward the mainland. Dicky, huffing up from the vanishing point and looking for all the world like a hairy testicle dressed in a suit and necktie,

pushes a stolen getaway car containing his mortally wounded partner, Albie (Jack MacGowran). Their talk has a distinctly Beckett-like rhythm.

Albie: I'm fed up.
Dicky: What about me?
Albie: It's digging into me.
Dicky: Where?
Albie: In my back.

Dicky relieves Albie's 'backache' by extracting a submachine gun from under him, as if it were a 30-pound iron splinter. He then notices a kite, fluttering trapped amid telephone wires. This inspires him to leave Albie behind for now, cross the grassy dunes and see about making a phone call from that castle. He spies a bare-breasted Teresa necking in the sand with a handsome youth and keeps moving. The castle abounds in chickens. Dicky sneaks in, hides, feasts on raw eggs (eggs being all

Still from 'Cul-de-Sac' (1966)
Critic Ivan Butler suggests that what we have
here is a playful allegory of British history,
embodied by George (named for England's saint
and dragon slayer), who suffers at the hands of
a pretty French conquest he cannot quite hang
onto, and a chummy American bully who
imposes himself from 'across the water'.

there are to eat) and spies on George, who comes up from another stretch of beach
bearing a box-kite.

So, this is whose kite hung above the highway. It is out of such teasing clues and
tiny, satisfying payoffs that Polanski and Brach construct their story; ten minutes in,
we know who these people are, and it has all been revealed in action. We might
overhear useful titbits of 'exposition' as we go (that Dicky and Albie screwed up a
robbery, or that George owned a factory before rescuing Teresa from a sordid life)
but these only provide backs to their heads. We are never offered explanations for
who they are. We can see that for ourselves.

While they think they are alone, Teresa and George engage in some cross-
dressing foreplay. She has (with subtle malice) pressed him to try on her negligee. At
first he only grudgingly obliges but, as she lines him with mascara and lipstick,
George melts into a mincing falsetto, as much to please her as tickle himself. This is
fitting, for it is he who will prove to be the 'female victim' in this topsy-turvy yarn.
Moments later, when they confront Dicky rooting through the kitchen, George
does not realize he is still sporting Teresa's negligee and make-up. Dicky takes this in
gruff stride, pinching George's cheek with brute condescension. Significantly, it is
here that Polanski gives the listening Teresa her first close-up in the picture, and one
of her few. Is she scared? Is she thrilling at George's humiliation? Finding her soul
mate in Dicky? We'll need the rest of the story to know for sure.

From there on, either Dicky heckles George, or Teresa caustically goads him to stand up to Dicky. When all three wade through the waist-deep tide to fish the dying Albie from his sunken car, even Albie belittles George. In his delirium, he screams "Doris!!!!!" (his wife's name) as he groggily stares up at George's lipsticked face. Later, coming to his senses and minutes from death, Albie snidely refers to George as "the queer".

The film's comedy grows out of its theatrical roots. The characters are dimly conscious of adopting roles (tough guy, lord of the manor, damsel in distress) to gain advantage. George's undoing is that he seems permanently miscast by fate, afflicted with stage fright under any of the masks he adopts. Dicky is at home with whomever he affects to be, be that a regal houseguest effusively praising George's taste in decor, or (in one of the film's funniest twists) pretending to be the new butler when George's old friends unexpectedly show up. Polanski's theatrical experience and his war-honed sense that we all play roles to stay alive intensifies these scenes, so much so that *Cul-de-Sac* blazes free of its roots in Beckett and Pinter and becomes, for cinema history, something wholly original. We are among people who are a captive audience to each other. They may conceal ulterior motives (Teresa seems to have a seductive agenda towards Dicky), but you cannot help wondering how much they have concealed from themselves. With this in mind,

On the set of 'Cul-de-Sac' (1966)
Prepping the 'hot foot' scene. Polanski wedges pages torn from 'PARIS MATCH' between Lionel Stander's toes as Dorléac watches in giddy recoil. He later had copies of the same issue specially imported for painstaking reshoots that were doubtless even more painful for the short-tempered Stander.

Polanski tends to stare with his camera. We are thus afforded an extra-vivid sense of the castle's layout; most viewers could draw an accurate map after the picture is over. We are also allowed a deeper insight into these people.

A bravura eight-minute sequence without cuts takes place on the beach. The three have just buried Albie. George and Dicky have set aside their hostilities and bond over a bottle of scotch. Teresa, jealous of their dawning friendship, dashes off naked to the sea. Dicky ignores her, preoccupied by hopes that Katelbach will come. When a plane passes low, he tries to flag it, firing his pistol. Nothing. The conversation turns to women. Dicky, having seen Teresa in the dunes, toys aloud with telling George about her infidelity. "Nah," he decides. "You're too square." George in turn confides that he found Teresa in a ...(he whispers the word). He is probably saying "brothel", but the ambiguity is nicer, the idea gaining power for being unspeakable. Teresa emerges from the sea, complains at having heard shooting, and the three go inside. The significance of this extended take is that at the film's midpoint, we are given a textbook happy ending, albeit prematurely. Nobody is in danger; Dicky and George become the lion lying with the lamb. That this occurs midway is a hint that such mercy is fleeting. We can dimly sense that the next time darkness falls, it will fall hard.

After the disruptive guests have intruded and been chased away, Teresa dons make-up and models a sexy dress before her mirror, girding up for an unpredictable showdown. Dicky is lying on a mat in the courtyard, getting his first sleep in 48 hours. George is likewise passed out a few paces away. Teresa slips twists of paper between Dicky's bare toes and lights them. He wakes up in a fury, hot-feet bicycling. He tackles Teresa, and whips her backside with his belt. When George wakes up and fights to defend Teresa, Dicky sends him flying. Moments later, while Dicky phones Katelbach, Teresa tells George, "He tried to kiss me." Thus provoked, George righteously clutches the pistol she has stolen from Dicky's coat. Meanwhile, Katelbach has cut Dicky loose; there will be no rescue. So Dicky orders George and Teresa to stay locked in the wine cellar until he has gotten far away. Now that it is no longer necessary, George finally stands up to Dicky, putting two lethal holes in him. "You killed *him*," Teresa sighs, as Dicky staggers away into the outer darkness. From her peculiar intonation, we can infer she hoped Dicky would overpower and

Still from 'Cul-de-Sac' (1966)
After they bury Dicky's accomplice, the three enjoy a drunken interlude on the beach at dawn. Polanski filmed this entire scene in a single, 8-minute shot. Movement and dialogue had to be timed with exceptional precision, to be certain that the plane overhead would soar past right on cue.

kill George, leaving her free. Dicky has just enough juice left in him to retrieve his submachine gun. Bullets fly as he staggers back and dies, causing George's car to explode. In the ensuing chaos, Teresa runs off with Cecil, a suave stranger who had come with George's old friends, earlier in the day. He has returned in his shiny Jaguar purely by chance to fetch a rifle he had left behind. "Aren't you coming with us?" he asks George, who simply laughs to himself hysterically.

Intruders dead, friends kicked out, Teresa gone, George dashes out in the dawn's half-light as the tide again comes in. With his shaved head, he has always eerily resembled the eggs which have proliferated in every corner of his household. In the film's final moment, he even perches in a fetal, eggheaded ball atop an enormous, egg-shaped rock, as if he were about to hatch a new self. He hollers "Agnes!!!"; his first wife. His cry echoes the dying Albie's exclamation of *his* wife's name. Perhaps this indicates that George is not far from death? More likely, it is a subtle thread linking him to Albie at a poetic level, for if one were to shave the moustache and hair from the elder gangster, he would, with his big birdy-beak, be a twin for George. Such a rhyming resemblance between opposites is never a coincidence in the Polanski universe. In *Cul-de-Sac*, it hints that we hate and fear in others what we most hate and fear in ourselves.

Filming had been hell. The actors fought, the weather was uncooperative and The Compton Group grew panicky at Polanski's uncompromising work habits.

Still from 'Cul-de-Sac' (1966)
Cold, turbulent weather and the island's isolation made for badly frayed tempers among the cast and crew. One outburst was caught on film, when Dicky attacks Teresa after the hot foot. Stander went overboard slapping Dorléac around, and later apologized.

On the set of 'Cul-de-Sac' (1966)
Timid George bravely slays his dragon, but only when it is finally, absurdly, no longer necessary.

Nevertheless, he emerged from this ordeal with precisely the film he had set out to make. He knew its bold mixture of comedy and tragedy was without precedent. From *Bonnie and Clyde* (1967) to *Pulp Fiction* (1994), the enormity of its influence is inescapable. The American Independent movement of the 1990s particularly abounds in hip, absurdist, ironical crime films that have either been directly inspired or made courageous by the example of *Cul-de-Sac*.

Polanski quickly moved on. While skiing in Austria's Arlberg valley, he was moved to remember the Tatras Mountains and the folklore he had been exposed to while hiding in their foothills as a boy. He and Brach had often spoken of writing a vampire movie. They were struck that Paris audiences so often laughed at horror movies. Polanski mused, "Why not make one they could laugh *with* rather than at?" An American producer named Martin Ransohoff crossed his path at about this time. Best known for *The Beverly Hillbillies* on TV, and *The Americanization of Emily* on film, Ransohoff bought the American distribution rights for *Cul-de-Sac*, and lined up a deal at MGM for what was then called *Dance of the Vampires*. In return, he asked for the right of final cut in the United States. Polanski, dazzled by this direct line into Hollywood, readily consented. In time, he would regret this; Ransohoff eventually shredded the vampire film, inflicted a clunky new title (*The Fearless Vampire Killers, or Pardon Me, But Your Teeth Are in My Neck*), redubbed the voices and added a cartoon prologue. Polanski's cut, and his original title, prevailed in every country but the United States, and was a smash hit in every country but the United States. This Faustian bargain with Ransohoff nevertheless brought one great good into his life;

Still from 'Cul-de-Sac' (1966)
Here is one of the most publicized images from
Polanski's canon, a superb icon of existential
isolation. In the context of George's particular
downfall, it never fails to pierce the heart, or
deepen one's sense of wonder.

the producer was adamant that actress Sharon Tate be cast in the plum role of the
innkeeper's daughter. Polanski resisted at first, but was thunderstruck at Tate's
beauty.

The Fearless Vampire Killers (1967) is, in its director's cut, Polanski's most light-
hearted film, though it is not fully a comedy. Call it a romantic thriller with a sense
of humour. Like *Mammals*, it opens in the snow, as a jingling sled approaches us
from the vanishing point. The haunting voices of Krysztof Komeda's gorgeous
choral score give way to howling wolves. Fierce dogs give chase as a professor of
vampire studies and his assistant (Jack MacGowran and Polanski) arrive in
Transylvania under a full moon and, half-frozen, stop at an inn whose occupants live
in dread of a terror they refuse to mention by name.

This opening locates us in an Eastern Europe so isolated, icebound, and
superstitious as to make whatever horror intrudes more real. Polanski's attempt to
spread frozen butter on frozen bread is an observant gag worthy of either Buster
Keaton or one who has lived in an ultra-cold climate with his senses open. Similarly,
a joke about Jewish vampires and their indifference to crosses would only occur to
one for whom being Jewish in a world of Christian mythologies is a matter of life

TOP LEFT
Still from 'The Fearless Vampire Killers' (1967)
Polanski often opens with an intriguing horizon, provoking us to ask that most suspenseful of basic questions: "Who goes there?"

LEFT
On the set of 'The Fearless Vampire Killers' (1967)
Being chased by savage dogs.

TOP
Still from 'The Fearless Vampire Killers' (1967)
Polanski conceived of Professor Abronsius (Jack MacGowran, left) as 'a snow-dusted Einstein'. Those glass bulbs are an ancient remedy for backache, and typical of Polanski's knack for grounding his fantasies in reality, the more bizarre the merrier.

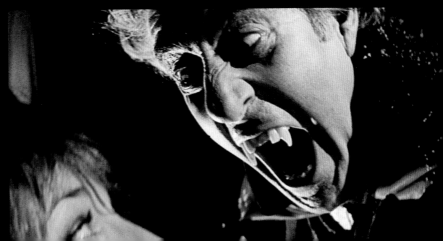

ABOVE
Still from 'The Fearless Vampire Killers' (1967)
Garlic everywhere. The professor asks, "Is there a castle in the district?" Shagal the innkeeper (Alfie Bass) is reluctant to say.

TOP RIGHT
Still from 'The Fearless Vampire Killers' (1967)
Count Krolock (Ferdy Mayne) attacks the innkeeper's beauteous, bubble-bath loving daughter, Sarah (Sharon Tate).

RIGHT
Still from 'The Fearless Vampire Killers' (1967)
Polanski doubted Tate could play a Jewish girl, but she screen-tested wonderfully (and donned a red wig to help the illusion). In the end, her sweet nature and high dedication won him over.

ABOVE
Still from 'The Fearless Vampire Killers' (1967)
Alfred (Roman Polanski) wants to tell the
professor that there is a vampire in the next
room, but cannot get the words out.

TOP RIGHT
Still from 'The Fearless Vampire Killers' (1967)
Later, as they stumble about the high parapets
of the Count's castle, Alfred maintains a slippery
foothold as he plucks an icicle from the
professor's nose.

RIGHT
Still from 'The Fearless Vampire Killers' (1967)
When he briefly has a chance to drive a stake
through the Count's heart, Alfred cannot do it.
(Too sweet; too squeamish.)

and death. Professor Abronsius and young Alfred notice the inn is encrusted with garlic. "Is there a castle in the district?" the professor asks, and his hosts gasp, refusing to answer. To not only bow to a tyrant but deny his existence is a ghoulish paradox so human one cannot help but feel hints of life under the Nazis intruding, like a ghostly chill. Alfred falls in love with the innkeeper's gorgeous daughter, Sara (Tate). She likes him, too, but while flirting with him from a high window, she catches the eye of Kukol (Terry Downes), the Count's dogged hunchback. As with George's lost kite, which attracts Dicky's eye in *Cul-de-Sac*, Polanski's people cannot help but call trouble their way. And Tate's hypnotic loveliness has the character of a supernatural provocation. Within a day, she is kidnapped from her bubble bath by Count Krolock (Ferdy Mayne) and taken to his castle. The professor and the lovesick Alfred pursue them over the snows and slip through the castle gates to save Sara. They are briefly made welcome as guests because Count Krolock has read the professor's books. Alfred continues courting Sara, whom he finds enjoying yet another bubble bath. He also dodges the amorous attentions of the Count's son (Iain Quarrier), "a gentle, sensitive youth", in his father's ironic description, who tries to put the bite on him. This leads to a Mack Sennett-style chase. Alfred and the professor then attempt to put a stake through the Count's heart but fail. The Count later puts them in their place when he has them cornered. "It will be my pleasure to fill in the gaps in your learning," he intones, "When you have attained my spiritual level." (Ferdy Mayne delivers this and all his other speeches with a charismatic force.) The Count does not see himself as a vampire. After all, evil does not see itself as evil. He prefers to regard himself as a pastor presiding over a flock, recruiting new adepts to his holy cause. His diabolical evangelism culminates with a ballroom ritual in which dozens of vampires rise from their graves after centuries of sleep, to dance a minuet and feast on Sara. Alfred and the professor infiltrate this party in disguise and are discovered but narrowly escape with Sara. In a lively chase, they elude capture by Kukol, who toboggans after them on a coffin. Their triumph is brief. Sara has been turned into a vampire. She sleepily opens her mouth as if to kiss Alfred, revealing a pair of fangs. He never sees them coming.

Polanski and Tate are so visibly falling in love on-camera that this final shocker can be heart-rending. He has created such a warm, sweet, Chaplinesque hero in Alfred that he is by far the most sympathetic character in the story. One can easily imagine that had the film not been butchered by Ransohoff, or had MGM released it with greater faith and care, Polanski might have found his way as an actor to the same public which was then embracing such cuddly gnomes as Dustin Hoffman and Woody Allen. As a director, he plays to the heightened emotion of this ghastly moment with a discreet cut. To see Alfred transformed into a vampire would be unmercifully depressing, so Polanski instead only shows his leg, thrashing as he is bitten. His slipper flips limply into the speeding snow and the Alfred we know has ceased to exist.

The professor's moustache and shock of white hair have styled him throughout

Still from 'The Fearless Vampire Killers' (1967)
Alfred must dodge the amorous advances of Count Krolock's "gentle, sensitive" son Herbert (Iain Quarrier).

"I am a happy man," Polanski would remember telling himself. Whatever agonies he suffered over the American release of *The Fearless Vampire Killers*, he was in love and in demand. He and Sharon moved in together. Paramount chief Robert Evans, a fan of *Cul-de-Sac*, heard Polanski was a passionate skier and lured him to Hollywood on the pretext of developing a ski picture for Robert Redford, *Downhill Racer*. The instant Polanski sat down, Evans handed him proof sheets of a novel that was about to be published. Would he take a look at this first? The novel was by Ira Levin. At first, Polanski thought Evans must be out of his mind; the opening pages were about Rosemary and Guy, a young married couple in love, taking a New York apartment in a building with a dark but colourful history. "Soap opera," he muttered. A page or so later, he was hooked. Sinister clues began to build. For the next several hundred pages, Rosemary is either losing her mind (owing to a painfully difficult pregnancy) or she is being used, against her will, by a coven of modern-day witches who wish her to give birth to the Antichrist. By the time Polanski turned the last page, it was four in the morning. His answer to Evans was "Yes."

Rosemary's Baby (1968) follows Levin's novel faithfully. "When Roman said it started like a soap opera," production designer Richard Sylbert later laughed, "He was actually stating the tone that made the story work." The opening credits are written as pink ribbons. Rosemary (Mia Farrow) can be heard, shyly singing a lullaby (composed by Komeda) that sounds like a dazed version of Doris Day's hit 'Que Sera, Sera'. Rosemary and Guy (John Cassavetes), freshly married and lyrically holding hands, tour the gothic Dakota apartments in mid-Manhattan. Guy is an ambitious actor. Rosemary, a devout Catholic, is eager to become a mother.

It is only by subtle but steady degrees that Rosemary, and we, come to suspect things are not right. Not right with her new neighbours, Minnie and Roman (Ruth Gordon and Sidney Blackmer), not right with the food she is eating, not right with Guy. There are ghastly little clues, like mute cries for help, left behind by the apartment's now-deceased previous tenant. Strange chanting can be heard at night through the walls to Minnie and Roman's apartment. A kind young woman Rosemary meets in the basement laundry room dies hours later – a suicide. Above all, there is the strange nightmare Rosemary has one evening at the fertile height of her monthly cycle. She and Guy were planning to conceive a baby, but Rosemary faints after eating a special dessert Minnie has prepared. In truth, she ate only half, hating its taste and so is actually half-awake later, when she finds herself naked on an altar-like bed, being savagely impregnated by a scaly superhuman. "This is no dream," she cries out. "This is really happening!!!" Guy explains the next morning that he made love to her while she was passed out. "I dreamt I was being raped by something inhuman," she tells him. He laughs: "Thanks a lot." From there, Rosemary's life becomes like a replay of Patrick Hamilton's classic drama, *Gas Light* (1938). Her every perception is either challenged or shot down, if not by Guy, then by Minnie and Roman. The instant she discovers she is pregnant, she becomes

Still from 'The Fearless Vampire Killers' (1967)
Sharon Tate and Roman Polanski fell in love while making this film. One can feel it in their scenes together. For all the wild darkness of the film's humour, they give it a warm heart.

TOP LEFT
Still from 'The Fearless Vampire Killers' (1967)
Quick, make the sign of the cross! Alfred and the professor hold the angry Count and his many dinner guests at bay while Sarah watches in a semi-trance.

LEFT
Still from 'The Fearless Vampire Killers' (1967)
Dance of the Vampires' was Polanski's original title, and that is what the film is called everywhere except the United States. For this is a dance, at heart, even before it is a comedy.

ABOVE
Still from 'The Fearless Vampire Killers' (1967)
Alas, Sarah is too far gone. Alfred is so in love with her, and so happy at the rescue he has just pulled off, that he cannot see the terrible bite she is about to put on him.

knows they are lying. She can hear its cries, right through the walls. In the film's final scene, she gathers her strength, locates the secret passageway to where her baby (whose inhuman face we never see) reposes in perfect health. She confronts the cabal of witches, spits on Guy, and is so taken aback with horror at her own baby's face that, at first, she must clap a hand over her own mouth to suppress a scream. "What have you done to his eyes???" she hollers at the witches. "He has his father's eyes," Roman tells her calmly, meaning Satan. "You don't have to join us, if you don't want to. Just be his mother." Rosemary takes a second look, and (motherhood being a mighty force) begins to rock the cradle. The lullaby repeats.

Stylistically, Polanski is in his element. With the full palette of Hollywood wizardry at his fingertips, he is fully enabled for the first time in his creative life to realize his twin passions for concrete realism and subtle, dreamily psychological distortion. (*Repulsion* was nothing if not a perfect dress-rehearsal for *Rosemary*.) Most of the action is restricted to Rosemary's floor in the Dakota (rechristened The Bradford), so Polanski enjoyed the rare freedom of filming in chronological order. This allowed Mia Farrow in particular to not just play Rosemary but to inhabit her. He also found Levin's novel so cinematic, right down to the terse brevity of its dialogue, that he was able to adapt it without co-writers. He also filmed virtually the whole book. His first fine-cut clocked at four hours, then editor Sam O'Steen distilled it to two hours and sixteen minutes. Such extraordinary inner freedom in turn freed Polanski to get psychologically detailed performances from his entire cast. Ruth Gordon's Minnie is a creepy marvel, birdlike in her physical delicacy, yet a menacing nuisance, and comic into the bargain. In terms of his body of work, *Rosemary's Baby* most closely hearkens back to his short film *When Angels Fall*. Both begin and end with a soaring view of city rooftops. In both, Polanski dramatizes a mystical experience in terms that he, a sceptic, can accept. In each case, it is the absolute nature of a mother's love for her child that calls forth the angelic encounter. Polanski's religious feelings died with his mother, yet twice in his work he has allowed that it is before a mother's deep connection with her offspring that he is still willingly humbled, and open to awe. That Levin's book so forcefully culminates in reconciliation between a mother and son must have touched a live nerve in Polanski's psyche. Small wonder he stayed up till dawn to finish the book.

Not long after filming concluded, he married Sharon Tate. Their wedding in London on 20 January 1968 was news around the world, and in Los Angeles they lived at the centre of a wide glittering circle that mixed old-time Hollywood stars with the industry's younger generation like Mia Farrow, Peter Sellers, Warren Beatty, Leslie Caron, Bruce Lee (who became Polanski's martial arts instructor) and Steve McQueen. Both groups would mingle freely at the large parties the couple threw.

Rosemary's Baby was an enormous hit, with lines around the block, and lucrative offers were pouring in. Polanski briefly returned to *Downhill Racer*, working with writer James Salter and inventing harnesses with which to shoot while in motion on skis. Alas, Paramount wanted him to film in the Rockies while he wanted the more rugged alps. In the end, it was directed by Michael Ritchie. Thus the year following the success of *Rosemary's Baby* offered Polanski his first chance to rest and reflect since he had entered film school. He was more relaxed now than he had been since the summer of 1939. He was particularly enamoured of the hippie movement, which was then in full flower. He told one interviewer. "For the first time in my experience, I hear young people speak about love and peace, and they really try to put it into practice."

"Optimism, a belief in yourself... seems an arrogance to many people because of this code of behaviour in our society that demands you to be humble... But this is essential to success, at least in certain endeavours, like film-making or seduction. It's like a war. It's necessary when you attack to be convinced that you're going to take the town, to be convinced that you're superior to the foe and that food and drink and women are in the town. It's inconceivable to take the town when your commanding officer tells you that you may take it, but then again, you may not, and even if you do, you have to go on to the next town before you find something to eat. So, especially when I'm making a film, I have to prepare myself for victory."

Roman Polanski

OPPOSITE TOP
Still from 'Rosemary's Baby' (1968)
Rosemary (Mia Farrow) and her husband Guy (John Cassavetes) get comfortable in their new apartment. Polanski and production designer Richard Sylbert relished the deceptive 'soap opera, romance-novel' atmosphere called for by the book's early chapters and at first replicated this feeling in the lighting, performances and mood, the better to lull viewers before socking them with the supernatural.

OPPOSITE BOTTOM LEFT
Still from 'Rosemary's Baby' (1968)
Ralph Bellamy as the avuncular, ultimately sinister Dr Sapirstein.

OPPOSITE BOTTOM RIGHT
Still from 'Rosemary's Baby' (1968)
Ruth Gordon, incomparably funny and creepy as Minnie Castevet, an emissary of Satan. She pressures Rosemary to regularly take a foul-tasting beverage, as well as wear an oddly stinky pendant on her neck.

Tate was for him the flower of flowers. They moved lightly about Los Angeles. A growing retinue of friends, some lonely, some freshly escaped from Poland, floated along with them. Polanski marvelled at Tate's instinctive generosity and hospitality. After a long day spent filming, she would think nothing of plunging into the kitchen to bake a ham or a cake. She would even insist on it. "She was kindness itself to everybody and everything around her – people, animals, everything," he would remember. "It's difficult to describe her character. She was just utterly good, the kindest human being I've ever met, with an extreme patience. To live with me was proof of her patience, because to be near me must be an ordeal." By early 1969, she was pregnant. She had had recently re-read her favourite novel, Thomas Hardy's *Tess of the D'Urbervilles* (1891). While passing through London, where Polanski was at work developing a thriller called *The Day of the Dolphin*, she gave him a copy. The dark fates that gather around the radiant Tess were in harmony with his war-hardened view of the universe, and Tess herself was an ideal part for Tate, who was otherwise being wasted in bimbo roles. Her innate luminosity as well as her delicate and intense emotional presence were qualities Polanski knew his skills could lay bare. Together, both agreed, they would create an unforgettable *Tess*.

Tate headed back to the United States early because the baby was due in August. Polanski was still in England late on Friday, 8 August, when he and Tate spoke long-distance. There was a snag regarding his visa – he could not come back to California until Monday. Tate was eager that he return. Their baby was about to be born and she needed him to gently clear their friends off the property before that happened. Earlier in the year they had rented a semi-rustic estate above Benedict Canyon in Los Angeles and, in typical style, were playing host to a cherished group, among them Abigail 'Gibby' Folger, a wealthy coffee heiress, her boyfriend Wojtek Frykowski (an old pal of Polanski's), as well as Jay Sebring, a top hair-stylist, who had been Tate's lover years before but was now one of Polanski's dearest friends. Although tongues would wag at the unusual intimacy of their three-way friendship (wrongly imagining it was sexually three-way), "The truth was that despite his material success and veneer of playboy self-assurance, Jay was fundamentally a gentle, lonely person who looked on us as his only real family." As much as they loved these friends, he was prepared to quietly evict them. He and Tate looked forward to being alone with each other and the new child.

On Saturday, the phone rang again. Polanski was surprised to find it was his friend and agent Bill Tennant. "There's been a disaster at the house," he said. "They've all been killed." Polanski could not quite comprehend what that meant. Did Bill mean a landslide? No, he replied. "They've all been murdered – Sharon, Jay, Wojtek, Gibby. All of them."

Still from 'Rosemary's Baby' (1968)
Our one direct glimpse of the baby's father. In an eye blink, Rosemary realizes, and unwittingly paraphrases Kafka's Gregor Samsa: "This is no dream – this is really happening!!"

ABOVE
Still from 'Rosemary's Baby' (1968)
About last night… Rosemary wakes up, her skin mysteriously cut, as if raked by sharp nails. Her actor husband is unconvincing in his overly smiley explanations.

LEFT
Still from 'Rosemary's Baby' (1968)
A circle of Satan's helpers ever so amiably drug Rosemary. Polanski, 'wholly in favour of typecasting', made detailed drawings of all the secondary characters in advance of production, and asked that actors be cast to match them.

ABOVE
On the set of 'Rosemary's Baby' (1968)
Polanski at a peak of unclouded happiness in
his life, working with exuberance and energy.
Mia Farrow is on the moving platform at left, for
the 'Sistine fresco' passage of Rosemary's
'dream' as she is ferried half-awake to the Black
Mass.

RIGHT
On the set of 'Rosemary's Baby' (1968)
Day by day, Farrow and Polanski bonded while
filming and became great friends. They kept
playful charts of one another's moods. Even
when Frank Sinatra cruelly sued her for divorce,
Farrow soldiered on.

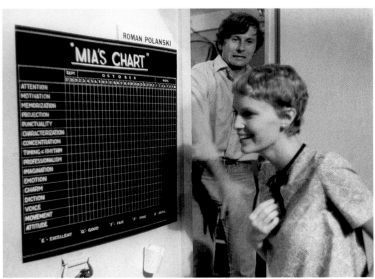

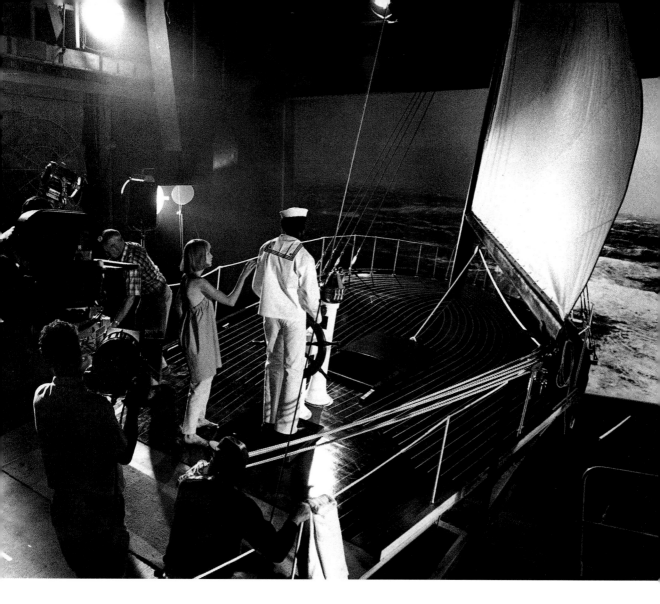

On the set of 'Rosemary's Baby' (1968)
Rear projection and other tricks of the trade,
circa 1968, are well orchestrated by Polanski to
create Rosemary's half-wakeful 'dream', as she
is taken to her Satanic impregnation.

Witches' Sabbath
1970–1978

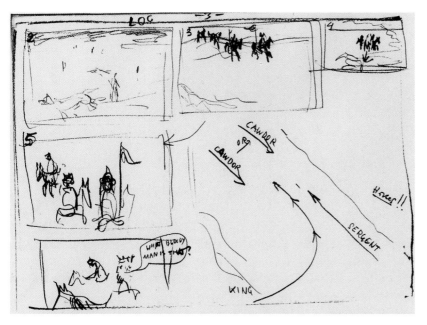

OPPOSITE TOP LEFT
Still from 'Macbeth' (1971)
After the opening titles, as mists clear and sounds of battle fade, one soldier claims the spoils of victory.

OPPOSITE TOP RIGHT
Still from 'Macbeth' (1971)
But the body he discovers twitches, and the lone soldier finishes him off.

OPPOSITE BOTTOM
Still from 'Macbeth' (1971)
"When the hurlyburly's done." The King rides through the coastal battlefield, a cruel landscape made beautiful by Polanski's eye for the wet, mirrored surface of the sands.

LEFT TOP
Storyboard for 'Macbeth' (1971)
Polanski's storyboard shows the opening scene with the lone soldier (panel marked '2') and the King riding through (panel 3). The diagram shows the relative positions and movements of the players: the sergeant; the King; and the Thane of Cawdor.

LEFT MIDDLE
On the set of 'Macbeth' (1971)
To film the king's entourage riding at speed along Portmadoc beach in North Wales, the cameraman poked through the sunroof of a small car hurtling parallel. Polanski is (where else?) in the driver's seat.

LEFT BOTTOM
On the set of 'Macbeth' (1971)
Horses, men, car and camera, all at full gallop.

PAGES 82/83
On the set of 'The Tenant' (1976)
The great founder of the French Cinémathèque, Henri Langlois (seated, deep background), dwarfed by the 'false perspective' of a set Polanski had built for a hallucination sequence.

"Sharon's death is the only watershed in my life that really matters," Polanski later wrote. Tate and their friends had been attacked just after midnight, following a quiet evening. They had been tied up, tortured, shot and butchered with knives. Amateurish symbols of devil-worship were scrawled in blood around their bodies. The first policeman on the scene was so rattled that he smudged the one clear thumbprint the killers left behind, as he desperately pumped the button at the electric gate to let himself out and radio for backup. The assailants were thus unknown for months. When he reached Los Angeles, Polanski's grief turned to rage when he discovered how his wife's memory and that of his friends were being buried by the news media, under an avalanche of the most vicious and sensationalist gossip. It was wrongly but widely reported that the victim's heads had been covered with hoods (as in a witches' cult), that they were semi-nude, that Tate's breast had been cut off, that the house was littered with drugs – myths that persist to this day. "God*damn* them!" Polanski would later rage. "They blamed the victims for their own murders." A magazine called *Pageant* headed their article, 'Those Sharon Tate Orgies – Sex, Sadism, Celebrities'. More bitterly offensive still was a widely syndicated article by Joe Hyams, 'Why Sharon Had To Die'. Hyams and his wife Elke Sommer inflated their single, sycophantic encounter with Polanski and Tate into a chronicle of intimate friendship.

By December, the police broke the case and arrested Charles Manson, a failed singer-songwriter who had spent most of his life in prison, but of late had gathered a

Still from 'Macbeth' (1971)
A mythic landscape, glowingly recreated. Miles of paved road were carefully and laboriously dressed to appear to be dirt tracks.

Still from 'Macbeth' (1971)
The coronation of Macbeth (Jon Finch). His bare feet are true to all primitive rites of elevation, which reiterate that a King is mortal, and must draw his strength from the earth, and society. Here is also a subtle foreshadowing, a striking tableau of all Macbeth will have to answer for, and to whom.

cult of young followers who shared a ranch with him in the San Fernando Valley. He nursed a deadly grudge against record producer Terry Melcher, the previous renter at the Tate house. Manson was a familiar pest to many luminaries in the record business; Brian and Dennis Wilson of The Beach Boys learned to their chagrin that he liked to come prowling around their homes with his followers at all hours. He felt cheated by life. He wanted revenge and he wanted money. After his friend Bobby Beausoleil had been arrested in early August on a murder charge, Manson ordered his 'family' to copycat that killing in an extreme way, down to such small details as leaving witchy inscriptions on the scene. The plan was to confuse the police and perhaps free Beausoleil. For the rest of it, Manson liked to proclaim himself both Jesus and the Devil Incarnate, and that he had had a prophetic vision while listening to the Beatles' *White Album*.

Polanski, expert enough at scaring large audiences to know a cheap trick when he smelled one, flatly dismissed this. "I think they were after money that night, and Manson was clever enough to know that if money came to be viewed as the motive, he wouldn't seem such a mystifying figure," he told Larry DuBois of *Playboy*. Years later, to Lawrence Weschler of *The New Yorker*, Polanski closed with another thought: "He was an artist spurned, and it can be a very dangerous thing to spurn a certain kind of artist. Think of Hitler."

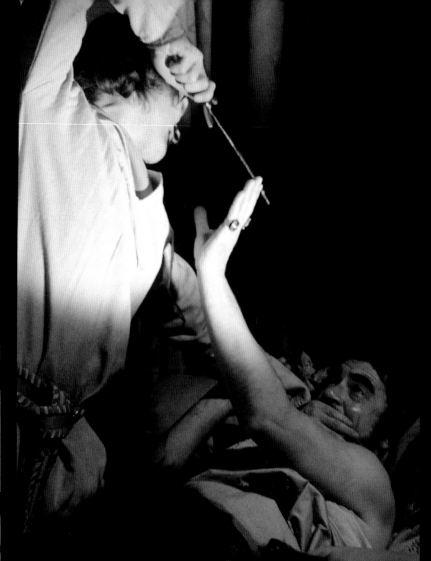

ABOVE
On the set of 'Macbeth' (1971)
Macbeth's murder of Duncan. Polanski shows
how to kill a king.

RIGHT
Still from 'Macbeth' (1971)
And Jon Finch shows how well he takes
direction.

With the killers securely behind bars, and the press now free to chew on
somebody else, Polanski recuperated in Switzerland, skiing himself into states of
exhaustion, avoiding the flood of paparazzi who followed him everywhere. He
unsuccessfully attempted to mount a production of the best-selling book *Papillon* by
Henri Charriere. The indomitable author's tales of his escapes from South America's
most hair-raising prisons reawakened Polanski's most positive spirits. He even got
Warren Beatty to say yes to playing the lead. Unfortunately, Walter Reade, the
theatre-magnate who owned the rights, had arbitrarily set a low budget from which
he would not budge. There was no way to achieve the book's thrilling scale for that
little and so this mouth-watering opportunity fell to the wayside. The good news
was that Polanski had begun to rebound. A comedy was out of the question. Even a
thriller would likely be pounced upon by the press. His imagination therefore lighted
on a long-ago daydream – a film based on a Shakespeare play. Why not rebound
from personal tragedy with a classical one?

Macbeth (1971) was a perfectly suitable choice and not because of its violence, or
Polanski's recent exposure to death, but because of what he now knew of life.
Contrary to tradition, he made the ambitious couple youthful and beautiful. As his

co-adaptor, critic Kenneth Tynan, put it: 'They do not know they're in a tragedy.' Is this a mirror image of how Polanski saw his own happiness with Tate, in retrospect? Certainly the mysteries at the heart of the play energized him and the result is a haunting, highly original take on a famously accursed drama.

Having Tynan on board as a script partner served two shrewd purposes. Renowned as 'a critic of genius', admired for his years of creative partnership with Laurence Olivier, Tynan's expertise naturally unlocked depths of the play that Polanski might miss, despite his many gifts. What is more, his involvement would defend it against cheap attacks, at least in Britain. "Roman," observed Tynan, "is a rigid purist where screenwriting is concerned. He absolutely forbids the vague, emotive stage directions (e.g., 'the atmosphere is threatening,' 'he seems uneasily preoccupied,') with which many scripts are padded. He insists that we confine ourselves strictly to what can be seen and heard. 'Anything else is cheating.' Example of his passion for concrete detail – we discuss a shot of the advancing English army, and he asks, 'Should they move right to left across the frame, or left to right?' I rashly say, 'Does it matter?' 'Of course it matters,' he says. 'To the Western eye easy or successful movement is left to right, difficult or failed movement is right to left.' He sends out for a children's comic to prove his point. On the first page a canoe is shooting the rapids left to right, and a man is climbing a mountain right to left. The English army moves left to right..."

"... His knowledge of all branches of film-making is daunting and encyclopaedic. In addition to dictating the choice of lens and camera angle, he supervises props, make-up, costumes and lighting. Many directors cover themselves by shooting sequences from several different angles, sometimes using three or more cameras. Characteristically, Roman prefers to go for broke, like a high-wire artist without a

LEFT
Still from 'Macbeth' (1971)
"Screw thy courage to the sticking place." Young, beautiful, deadly ambitious Lady Macbeth (Francesca Annis) steels herself for her own role in King Duncan's murder.

BELOW
Still from 'Macbeth' (1971)
"What is that noise?" Why, that would be Lady Macbeth, sir, hurling herself to her death.

net. He hardly ever uses more than one camera, and he favours long takes on which he must stake everything, since this method makes it impossible for him to delete anything without causing an unacceptable jump-cut. Having committed himself to a single camera setup, he lets the takes multiply. The crew [mimicking his Polish accent] already echoes his refrain – 'That's mudge bedder, beautiful. *Once again!*'"

Tynan's synopsis of the plot is revealing of their interpretation: "When the witches prophesy that Macbeth will be King, he is filled with exhilaration, like a man who has come into an unexpected fortune. That is the dream. Rushing to fulfil it, the Macbeths encounter the reality of their own natures, which hitherto neither of them knew. And that is the tragedy." Macbeth's murder of the rightful King, Duncan, was designed by Shakespeare to take place offstage, because the playwright knew his own King, James, would be sitting in the audience. Polanski laboured under no such obligation. As Macbeth (Jon Finch) steals into Duncan's bedchamber, he gazes upon his kind face and hesitates, daggers in hand. The fit of nagging conscience in his eyes is a silent soliloquy. Then the King stirs, as if feeling the malign presence in his dreams, and the two men gaze directly at one another. Macbeth is now so ashamed (as well as guilty) that he falls on Duncan with a triggered savagery. Wherever possible, Polanski amplifies Shakespeare's text with imaginative but appropriate staging. Another fine sequence comes late in the action as Macbeth, now King, is tormented by bad dreams of his friend Banquo, whom the witches prophesied would father a race of Kings. In Macbeth's nightmare we revolve through an endless parade of unknown Kings on future thrones, each seated beside empty mirrors in which Macbeth can make out no reflection – only more and more new Kings, who in no way resemble himself. A more controversial invention had Lady Macbeth sleepwalking nude as she guiltily seeks to erase that "damned spot" from her hands. No one wore pyjamas in the middle ages, and it is carried off tastefully, but the scene provoked puritanical howls of outrage in America. Aristotle's unities are upheld by treating the entire story from Macbeth's viewpoint, apart from a brief prologue and epilogue involving the witches. Even when his head has been severed and stuck on a pike, we get a chilling point-of-view shot. Macbeth is not quite dead. The axe's blow has deafened him, and he now views the fading world upside-down as he is carried on the pike-tip through the madly joyful crowd. It is an unforgettable moment of damnation, seen from the inside.

Polanski resented any attempt to depict his *Macbeth* as a catharsis. "They are full of shit," he said of such critics. For him, Shakespeare was the attraction. If anything, the violence, the weaponry, the bits of sport (bear-baiting, a barefoot peasant-dance amid daggers), hearken not to his recent past, but to his 'medieval' boyhood in Wysoka. (The film's opening shot of horizons layered in mist could be a postcard of the Tatras foothills.) Moreover, he is out to communicate that blood-thirst which shadows every civilization. The memory of a Nazi officer flicking a crop to and fro, as he examined Polanski's teddy bear in the Kraków ghetto, fed directly into the cool malice of the soldiers who kill Macduff's children. Not as catharsis, but as an internal authentication. Similarly, when Tynan questioned the huge amount of blood being used to show the aftermath of this massacre, Polanski replied bleakly, "You didn't see my house in California last summer." This, Tynan noted, was the only time in the year of their work together that he ever mentioned the tragedy, although there was one ironic shiver when Polanski gently daubed stage blood onto the face of a four-year-old girl playing one of the dead Macduffs, and asked her name. She replied, "Sharon."

ABOVE
Still from 'Macbeth' (1971)
The film begins with the witches at the beach. As is true of so many Polanski films, this one comes full circle and ends as it began, in this case with the witches. We even glimpse yet another fortune-seeking warrior of middle rank, seeking their advice.

OPPOSITE TOP
Still from 'Macbeth' (1971)
The forces amass against Macbeth.

OPPOSITE BOTTOM
Storyboard for 'Macbeth' (1971)
Polanski's drawings coordinate the clash. Kenneth Tynan, co-adaptor the screenplay, noted that Polanski designs all onscreen movement conscious that Western audiences read left to right. An army charging to the right thus implies more victorious strength than one moving against our mind's resistance, to the left.

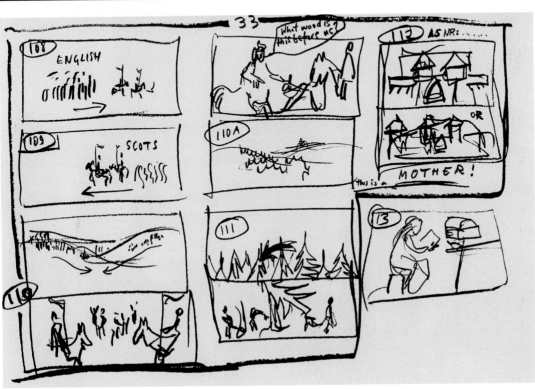

OPPOSITE
On the set of 'Macbeth' (1971)
To capture the unique light of the Welsh location for a particular interior, Polanski (waiting and watching, centre) built a room favouring a leaded-glass window, through which to grab the shot.

ABOVE
On the set of 'Macbeth' (1971)
"Macduff was from his mother's womb untimely ripp'd!" This final battle between Macbeth and his foretold vanquisher, Macduff (Terence Bayer) was filmed on a soundstage, where Polanski had time to choreograph the large number of actors and extras without prohibitive location costs.

ABOVE
Still from 'What?' (1973)
Nancy (Sydne Rome) is an upbeat young nomad
who finds herself a target for every predatory
male on the planet, which is to say every male,
period, including this Kerry Blue who wants her
t-shirt.

OPPOSITE TOP
Still from 'What?' (1973)
While escaping a knot of would-be attackers on
the road, she stumbles into a chateau full of
lusty eccentrics, led by Alex (Marcello
Mastroianni) who begs her to beat him. Her
most precious possession is her large quarto-
sized diary, which she totes with her everywhere.

OPPOSITE BOTTOM
Still from 'What?' (1973)
Her wardrobe is quickly reduced to that of a
single borrowed pyjama top, and the minute
does not pass that she is not importuned by yet
another noxious suitor.

For Playboy Enterprises, created by Hugh Hefner, *Macbeth* marked a maiden
foray into movie-making. Sad to say, their bravery backfired when weather on the
Welsh coast (gale force winds, slashing rains) added twelve weeks to a tightly
budgeted schedule. The other backlash was that, in their innocence, they opened the
film in New York instead of London, and in January rather than in the spring, when
they would surely have enjoyed a more effective launch. Worse, the American critics
preferred their still-fresh memories of Sharon Tate to their patchier grasps of
Shakespeare, and so pilloried both *Playboy* and Polanski. British critics, too late,
focussed on the freshness of the interpretation; 'Macbrilliant' read one headline.

What? is an erotic entertainment Polanski quickly wrote (with Brach) and filmed
in the summer of 1972. Call it a cinematic vacation from care, fear, shame and
repression. The heroine (Sydney Rome) is an indestructible innocent who wanders
into a Riviera chateau, loses her clothes and repeatedly dodges seduction as she finds
herself the toy in every perverse game the place's many denizens can devise.
Foremost among these is Marcello Mastroianni, as a hobbyist pimp, and Hugh
Griffith as his wealthy, mortally ill father. Polanski and Brach designed a witty
structure – the story spans two days, and the new day in this heavenly corner of
Hell hopelessly repeats the previous one. "Do you believe in *déjà vu?*" the heroine is
asked, twice, under identical circumstances. Sad to say, that is *What?*'s best line. The
rest of the dialogue tries hard to be as funny without success. Mastroianni is a great
natural clown, but spins in a vacuum for tedious stretches. Griffith and Rome fare

ABOVE
Still from 'What?' (1973)
The most human connection she makes is with the villa's dying patriarch, Noblart (Hugh Griffith), who asks her to stand astride his deathbed and indulge a last wish. "What splendour," he sighs, as she peels open her pyjama top.

RIGHT
On the set of 'What?' (1973)
Sydne Rome and Hugh Griffith assume their positions as Polanski directs. He and long-time collaborator Gérard Brach wrote the script, and made the film cheaply on the Italian Riviera.

better, sharing a sweet moment at the climax, as he lays dying. He asks her to stand over him, open her borrowed pyjama top (her only garment, by now) and let him have a peek between her legs. His plea is so childlike and heartfelt that she tolerantly complies. We never see what he sees – Rome's calves and thighs tower like twin colossi in the foreground. Griffith owns the moment with his vulnerable, ecstatic face, gazing up at the only vision of paradise Polanski could at that point in his life freely endorse. This is the film's most comic moment and its most poignant. After this, there is little for the heroine to do but grab her diary, lose her pyjama entirely, and (in the interest of Aristotelian unity) escape the chateau in a symmetric reversal of the way she came in. She rides off into the night, with only her diary to cover her, huddled aboard a deafening truckload of snuffling pigs, shouting the film's title over and over as Mastroianni begs her to return. Whatever its defects, *What?* is cheerful and unpretentious, less a film than a pastry, a sweet thing of dubious nutritional value designed to be consumed with lust (or so the chef hopes) in the course of one contented sitting. Critics at the time derided it as unworthy of Polanski. He did not care. It was cheap to do, and fun, and he was lightly enabled to make exactly the film he had in his head at that moment.

This whimsical escape also cleared his inner pipelines for a masterpiece. A fascinating screenplay, written by Robert Towne, had been commissioned by Paramount chief Robert Evans a couple of years before. Towne was respected throughout Hollywood; he had made fundamental contributions to both *Bonnie and Clyde* (1967) and *The Godfather* (1972). Evans had asked him to dinner to offer him the assignment of adapting F. Scott Fitzgerald's *The Great Gatsby* (1925), but Towne said no. He was consumed with a detective story. He then wove a spell, filling Evans' ears with tales of 1930s Los Angeles and the violent, rich, corrupt battles over water rights that created the city. He also had in mind a hero. This man would be a seasoned detective, superficially in the manner of Dashiell Hammett's Sam Spade and Raymond Chandler's Philip Marlowe, but with a romantic temperament closer to (interesting coincidence) Fitzgerald's Jay Gatsby. For J.J. Gittes, as Towne christened him, is, like Gatsby, a stylish and sociable go-getter with a thirst for big success. He just happens to be making his fortune as a private eye specializing in lucrative divorce cases. He is in high demand, makes good money and is thus ripe to be blindsided when a case comes along that seduces him into the heart of darkness. As Towne foresaw it, Gittes would find himself a captive witness to the heroic struggle of one woman, Evelyn Mulwray, to save her young daughter from the clutches of her murderous, child-abusing, politically well-connected father, Noah Cross. Evelyn had been molested by Cross. Her daughter is *his* daughter, and this is the secret Gittes must literally slap out of her, simply to make sense of what is going on, and understand the enormity of the danger both he and Evelyn are in.

This was the script Evans showed Polanski, at a tangled but incandescent 180 pages. Polanski was in awe of Towne's extraordinary ability to evoke character, inner life and outer atmosphere with such dazzling economy. There were only two problems: the subplots led in too many directions; and the ending was too sentimentally romantic. He and Towne solved the first problem by honing and pruning the script over a period of eight weeks. The second issue was more divisive. Towne had written that Evelyn would kill her father and in a romantic act of self-sacrifice go to jail, to set their daughter free. Polanski argued that Evelyn should die, murdered at her father's tacit behest. "Wrong, immoral, not the story I wrote," Towne replied, but Polanski was adamant: "That's what 'unforgettable' is all about."

Still from 'What?' (1973)
Nancy leaves the villa as she entered, running swift and madly clutching her diary, which is now her only covering. "What?" she cries out repeatedly to Alex, who pleads with her out of earshot as she rides naked into the night. "What?? What???"

For all the fury of their disagreement, *Chinatown* (1974) is the greatest popular and critical success of Towne's career, thus far, and (with the possible exception of *The Pianist*), Polanski's as well. Every now and then, fate conspires with a set of film-makers to get everything just right. Evans was at the height of his game as a producer. Towne's romantic faith in Evelyn as a heroine whom he was convinced must not die, matched against Polanski's blood-earned knowledge that life and love are governed by loss, made for a subliminal tension that brings both Evelyn and Jake more brilliantly to life. It also does not hurt that Jack Nicholson, who plays Jake, is at his most beautiful, while Faye Dunaway, who plays Evelyn, is at her most glamorous and inscrutable, or that John Huston, who plays Noah Cross, is so magnetic, merry and terrifying that he makes evil look like grand fun.

Polanski fused the story into sharply economical visual sequences. The very first shot shows a set of lurid black & white stills being riffled, one by one, so quickly that the sex act therein jumps rudely to life. Curly, the aggrieved husband of the woman caught copulating in these photos, bites back furious tears as Jake urges him to stay calm. Each move of the camera is as clean as a declarative sentence. Jake is hired to shadow the city's water commissioner, Hollis Mulwray. With him, we follow the man through his mysterious day: probing the dried bed of the Los Angeles river; questioning a young Mexican boy who clip-clops past on a swaybacked horse; and lingering by a drainage pipe near the Pacific ocean. Polanski (in collaboration with cameraman John Alonzo) films these bits for a maximum yield of information. They pan simply, leading our gaze across the massive, stylish span of an art deco bridge (archetypal Los Angeles architecture), following Mulwray's long 1920s Packard as he moves along the riverbed, continuing until Jake's sharp nose cuts into the picture in foreground close-up, revealing him at work, watching through binoculars.

One of the more agreeable pressures Polanski brought to Towne's final rewrite was an insistence that the entire film unfold strictly from Jake's point of view. If he is not there for an event, neither are we. The resulting intensity is akin to an intricate tracking shot without cuts. In this, the entire film becomes a 'complex master' of life inside the head of J.J. Gittes. There are, as Polanski admitted to students at the American Film Institute, "little cheats". We have a close-up of Evelyn, on the trembling verge of confessing her terrible secret in that narrow instant after Jake has driven away in anger from their first meal at the Brown Derby – a tragic near-miss, in retrospect. We get a telling close-up of her father, Noah Cross, as his back is briefly turned to Gittes during their later meal at his ranch. Gittes has just told him he knows about the "hell of an argument" Cross had with Mulwray two days before his murder. Cross' face falls wonderfully at this news, honestly surprised that he has been found out. Yet as much as these fleeting moments happen outside of Jake's immediate sight lines, they are a part of the puzzle he has so logically put together (to his everlasting horror) by the end of the film.

In relation to Polanski's other films, *Chinatown* may seem less personal because it began as an assignment. Yet he chose Faye Dunaway because her 'retro beauty' so recalled his late mother. (Her plucked eyebrows and cupid's-bow lipstick in the film are, he said, imitative of his mother's style.) That he and Dunaway so often fought at the tops of their voices while creating Evelyn is only proof of the depth of his own emotional investment in the character. The final result is so informed by Polanski's own memories of the 1930s that he fully earns co-authorship with Towne.

The shock and honesty of its incest theme have given *Chinatown* a long life, but

Still from 'Chinatown' (1974)
Writer Robert Towne and director Polanski dispense with cliche 'movie detective' voiceover, yet rigorously lock the story into the silent, observant viewpoint of Jake Gittes (Jack Nicholson, not shown). Here, Jake spies through binoculars as Hollis Mulwray (Darrell Zwerling) explores a dry riverbed.

in terms of its large, word-of-mouth success in the summer of 1974, Polanski's lucid, audience-friendly direction are crucial. If, as D.W. Griffith said, "The motion picture camera photographs thought", Polanski had over his career evolved a visual vocabulary which invites an audience to think along. Here, we enjoy a crowded canvas of heroes and predators whose thoughts we seem to be reading as they try with such stealth to outwit one another. A more topical reason for the film's success cannot be underrated, either. Richard Nixon became the first U.S. President ever to resign from office, less than three weeks after *Chinatown* opened. Many Americans (many of whom had voted for Nixon, a year and a half earlier) were reeling from the evidence that their leader was running an organized crime ring out of the White House. Polanski, Towne and Evans had, by grace of the fates, created a film which made poetic and tragic sense of such revealed corruption. Aristotle's idea that great drama calls an audience forth to feel the triple catharsis of pity, terror and awe, was and remains fulfilled by this unexpected masterpiece.

Polanski left for Europe before the film's release to direct a production of Alban Berg's opera *Lulu* in Spoleto, Italy. His next picture, he hoped, would be a frolic he called *Pirates*. As with *Cul-de-Sac*, he and co-writer Brach had cooked up a big buffet of their favourite kinds of scenes: adventurous, slapstick and swashbuckling. As with *Mammals* and *The Fat and the Lean*, there would be a Master and his Man Friday, but this time they are stranded on a raft, a minuscule speck in the middle of an infinite ocean. Jack Nicholson agreed play Captain Red, a farcical caricature of the

ABOVE
Still from 'Chinatown' (1974)
A knife in the actor. The Man with Knife (Roman Polanski) does the honours as Jake Gittes (Jack Nicholson) is pinned by Claude Mulvihill (Roy Jenson) and threatened with the loss of his nose.

PAGE 100
On the set of 'Chinatown' (1974)
Jack Nicholson is wetted down for his climb up the reservoir fence.

PAGE 101
Still from 'Chinatown' (1974)
Before cameras rolled, Nicholson grinned and held up one finger, mouthing the word: "One." One take only. For he was performing his own stunt, getting smashed against a fence by a deluge of water. Polanski made sure they got it in one.

PAGES 102/103
Still from 'Chinatown' (1974)
The dead eyes of Jake Gittes.

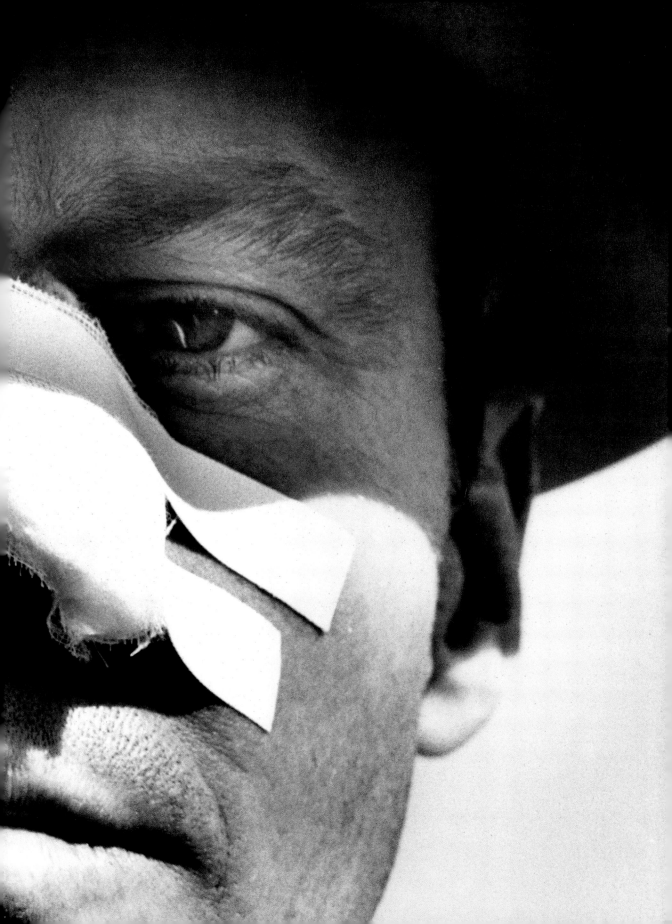

ABOVE
On the set of 'Chinatown' (1974)
Gittes searches for clues in the drought-parched orchard country north of Los Angeles. Note the yellow smoke to give texture to the air around the actors. Polanski, left of centre, wears a straw hat and shorts.

RIGHT
On the set of 'Chinatown' (1974)
Polanski shows an actor how he wants him to move with a crutch.

OPPOSITE
Still from 'Chinatown' (1974)
The farmers know they are being systematically robbed of water, mistake Gittes for one of their enemies and give him a beating. Even the guy on crutches gets in a few licks.

infamous Blackbeard, and Polanski would play The Frog, Red's loyal flunky. For the beautiful aristocrat they kidnap, he cast a stunning new French actress, Isabelle Adjani. A comedy involving Polanski and Nicholson? This was catnip to Paramount. *Pirates* nearly got made in this form in 1975. One can only wish it had been. Unfortunately, because he was trying to set it up through a company he had created, the better to stay in legal and financial control, negotiations between Paramount and the European backer Polanski had lined up became hopelessly muddled. Both the deal and the idea were shelved for the time being. Paramount had meanwhile acquired a novel by French cartoonist Roland Topor (creator of *Fantastic Planet*), and the instant Polanski read it, he expressed interest. Eight months later, he delivered the film. "I finished shooting it before even the contracts were signed."

The Tenant (*Le Locataire*, 1976) is a harrowing psychological thriller, a sibling of *Repulsion*. He cast himself as Trelkovsky, the Kafkaesque hero who is so affected by the suicide of the unknown woman who previously inhabited his apartment that, by slow degrees, he dons her abandoned clothes and takes on her self-destructive demons. She becomes the 'tenant' inside his head. Or is he the 'tenant' in hers? Does Trelkovsky even exist? The nightmarish ending is ambiguous enough to support both conclusions. Polanski has never been more nakedly, more singly intense than he is here. The opening credits boast a complex master to rival anything in *Touch of Evil* (1958). We see Polanski's face (or is it a woman's? French actress Dominique Poulange appears in glimpses throughout the film as the previous tenant, Simone Choule) peering at us from the shadows within one window. Without cuts, we soar to all the other windows in the building, lingering for an extra moment at the bathroom whose spooky Egyptian cuneiforms will assist in our protagonist's breakdown. To have achieved this shot in the days before either Steadicam or digital enhancement were developed is a feat of the most balletic precision. As the story begins, Trelkovsky is already living in a universe that fosters paranoia, alternately ignored or menaced by his building's concierge (Shelley Winters). Polanski and cameraman Sven Nykvist frame antic patterns in the snail-spiral of stairs which ascend to Trelkovsky's flat. Hooked by the tale of his predecessor's suicide, shocked that her clothes are still in his closets, intrigued that she is still hospitalized (though not expected to live), Trelkovsky pays her a visit. There he bonks foreheads with her friend Stella (Isabelle Adjani). They attempt to speak to her, but after one look at Stella (or is it Trelkovsky she recognizes?), the heavily-bandaged patient opens her mouth in a terrible scream. Trelkovsky's gaze travels into that open howl as if plunging down a rabbit hole into infinite darkness.

After this, Trelkovsky's command of reality grows more tenuous. Stella is attracted to him, and he lets her make seductive overtures, but he is increasingly listless in response. His buddies at work push him around. (In this, he is more like the tragic boyfriend in *Repulsion* than the heroine.) Sinister neighbours (among them Jo Van Fleet) try to embroil him in their cryptic quarrels. The apartment's owner (Melvyn Douglas) repeatedly accuses him of making a terrible racket in his apartment, when for all we know he is quiet as a mouse. There is one ambiguous clue, after he begins to cross-dress, that Trelkovsky and his demons are actually conducting loud orgies in his bed, but these are as much subject to erasure as the mysterious Egyptian writings he discovers in the toilet, across the courtyard. Eventually, when he can take no more, Trelkovsky, dressed as a woman, throws himself from the same window ledge the previous tenant did. He must even do so

Still from 'Chinatown' (1974)
Jake makes love to the mysterious Evelyn Cross Mulwray (Faye Dunaway) but when he suspects she is playing him for a fool, is reduced to slapping the truth out of her.

twice. When he comes to (or is he a 'she' now?) he is mummified beyond recognition in a head-to-toe body cast. He sees himself at the bedside shyly bonking foreheads with Stella, just as he did at the start of the story. This time when the tenant screams, the camera dives into his/her open mouth and does not come back.

The Tenant flopped but his career was unscathed. Polanski began to consider more commercial ideas but he was conscious of drifting. After half a decade, the loss of Sharon Tate still cursed his love-life. He could not bear the thought of a long-term relationship again; his years with her had simply been too happy. Just as troublesome was his awareness that most of the women available to him were actresses or film artists attracted to his power, who wanted something from him. He preferred to dally with teenagers, albeit sexually mature (their ages averaging from 16 to 19), whose primary appeals were their unspoiled beauty and an absolute indifference to his status in the world of movies.

Such consensual flings, so common in Europe as to cause no ripple, landed Polanski in deep trouble in the United States. On 10 March 1977, he had sex with a model he was photographing on what he had understood (owing to a verbal agreement) to be an assignment for French *Vogue*. Samantha Geimer by all accounts looked 18 or older, but her actual age, 13, triggered a riot of tabloid righteousness which persists to this day in any account of Polanski's doings. His unsparing autobiography, taken side-by-side with the girl's no less blunt court testimony, make painful reading. Polanski thought he was being seductive; Geimer was physically mature, comfortable posing nude, compliant in response, and was the ward of a 'liberated' mother and stepfather who both approved of the nudity and dismissed any need to chaperone her. By contrast, Ms Geimer did not feel seduced as much as cornered. She wanted to impress the big director from Europe, did not want to say the wrong thing and, much as she was already sexually experienced, felt nervous and out of her depth. She cut the evening short once the sex ended by faking an asthma attack.

And she was 13. (Born on 31 March 1963, she was three weeks shy of 14 at the time of the incident.) Polanski, though surprised at his arrest two days later, cooperated with the authorities. He confirmed Geimer's story. He was shaken that her feelings in the matter were so different from his, but readily accepted responsibility. Lawyers wrangled over the exact language of the charges, and judgement was held off for months in the hope that the publicity would cool. Polanski pleaded guilty to unlawful sex with a minor – case closed. Because no force was used, and because it was a first-time offence, Polanski's penalty might reasonably have been restricted to probation and a large fine, most importantly in the form of damages paid, to be held in trust for Ms Geimer. Unfortunately, the wealth of ugly headlines so rattled the Judge, Laurence J. Rittenband, that over the course of the next several months he blew hot and cold over whether to simply punish Polanski or make a special example of him.

Judge Rittenband ordered Polanski to enter Chino, a maximum security prison north of Los Angeles, for 90 days of psychological tests. In all the hubbub that has dogged his subsequent exile, it is generally forgotten that Polanski actually went to prison. "People in here are willing to kill you for a little publicity," he was told by one official on his first day inside. But he got through it, volunteering for cleanup detail by way of getting extra exercise. He was also grateful for the assurance that these months would be the worst of his punishment. Judge Rittenband had told Polanski's lawyer in chambers that his time in Chino would settle the question of

OPPOSITE
On the set of 'The Tenant' (1976)
Polanski built a vast indoor set, as Alfred Hitchcock did for 'Rear Window'. Using a Louma crane, the camera glides dazzlingly from window to window during the title sequence. That large mirror is crucial to both the focus and illusion of mobility he was after. A clever effigy of Polanski can be made out dimly in the last window on the right.

ABOVE
Still from 'The Tenant' (1976)
Trelkovsky (Roman Polanski), a Kafkaesque nebbish, moves into an apartment but the walls are paper-thin, and it is the sort of place where the neighbours complain if you sneeze too loud. Here he carefully lifts his table so that the tenants below do not hear him move furniture.

BELOW
Still from 'The Tenant' (1976)
Even his own rubbish rebels against him, dropping all over the stairs as he carries it, only to vanish before he can clean it up.

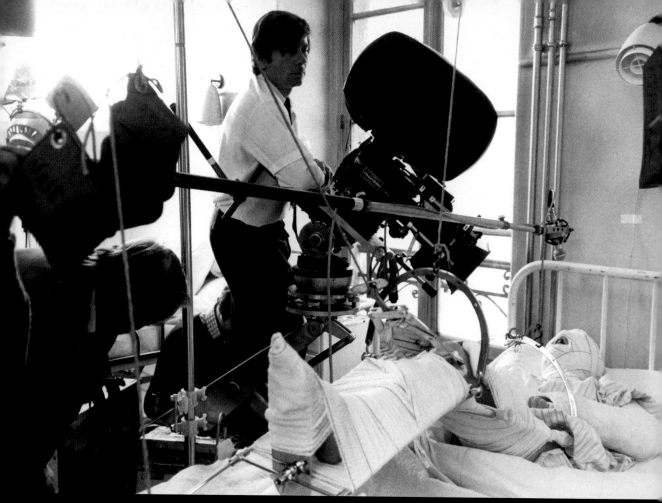

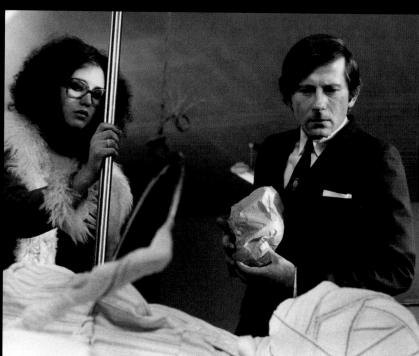

ABOVE
On the set of 'The Tenant' (1976)
Cameraman Sven Nykvist (lower left) and
Polanski (centre) take a close-up of Simone
Choule (Dominique Poulange) who previously
occupied Trelkovsky's apartment before throwing
herself out the window.

RIGHT
Still from 'The Tenant' (1976)
When Stella (Isabelle Adjani) comes to visit her
dying friend, she takes a fancy to Trelkovsky, but
he is far more fascinated by the poor bedridden
woman, who is otherwise unknown to him.

prison and what remained would be the fine and probation. Psychiatrists tested Polanski. After 42 days they recommended he be set free and he was. They reported that he was neither a paedophile nor a pathological sex offender. He was a clinically normal adult male who had made an appalling choice when he should have known better. Judge Rittenband waxed angry, having closely followed the headlines while Polanski was away. He was even checking up on clippings from overseas. When Polanski appeared before him again, the day after being released from prison, Rittenband suddenly reneged on his earlier deal and announced he was ordering him back to Chino for "an indefinite time period", which could mean days, weeks or years.

He then offered Polanski a second deal: he could be set free after 47 more days in prison by volunteering to have himself deported. Polanski, reeling, thought: 'Why wait?' That afternoon, he boarded a jet for Europe.

ABOVE
Still from 'The Tenant' (1976)
One man and a wardrobe – the unknown woman's clothes fill his closets. After she dies, he tries them on, until this ghostly woman becomes a tenant in his head. Or is he the tenant in hers?

PAGE 112
On the set of 'The Tenant' (1976)
When the overload of delusion and paranoia fostered by his hostile neighbours becomes too unbearable, he dons his predecessor's clothes and repeats her fatal leap. Twice!

PAGE 113 TOP
On the set of 'The Tenant' (1976)
Polanski used stand-ins (one is on the floor behind him) so he could juggle his double role as actor and director.

PAGE 113 BOTTOM
Still from 'The Tenant' (1976)
Trelkovsky sees his neighbours as monsters (Jo Van Fleet is Madame Dioz at left, Melvyn Douglas is Monsieur Zy at right).

In Flight, On Reflection, At Sea
1979–1986

ABOVE
Still from 'Tess' (1979)
Tess has a baby by Alec, but the child does not
survive.

RIGHT
Still from 'Tess' (1979)
The love struck but self-serving Angel Clare
(Peter Firth) has already ferried two other girls
across this flooded lane, all so that he could
have a chance to carry Tess third, and hold her.

PAGES 114/115
On the set of 'Pirates' (1986)
After the triumph of 'Tess', the grind of getting
films depressed Polanski, but when the
opportunity arose to make 'Pirates', he leapt.

PAGE 116 TOP
Still from 'Tess' (1979)
Maidens dance, an ancient, pagan rite ideal for
introducing Tess (Nastassja Kinski, right).

'Polanski Flees' read the headline on the late edition of *The Los Angeles Times*. As of this writing, Polanski has never returned to the United States. As he reflected on what had just happened, and cast about for a project that might renew his spirits, he returned to the book Sharon once asked him to adapt and direct for her.

Tess of the D'Urbervilles begins with a fatal conversation. A pompous country pastor greets Durbeyfield, the village drunk, by calling him "Sir John". When Durbeyfield challenges this, the parson smiles. "It was only my whim." He is a scholar of local families and has discovered that Durbeyfield is descended from the D'Urbervilles, a noble line dating back to William the Conqueror. The poor drunk goes mad with pride at this news. He presses his beautiful daughter, Tess, to contact the wealthy branch of the D'Urbervilles. (These are a false branch of the line, who bought their title from the Durbeyfields a few generations back.) Tess obediently makes their acquaintance, only to fall prey sexually to Alec, the roguish heir. This impregnating cataclysm ends hundreds of pages later with Tess being led away to the gallows. All from what the smug parson so teasingly described as "just a whim of mine".

The novel's tragic afterimage burns particularly bright because Tess is such an innately noble character. In her refusal to cave in to self-pity, she emerges as a *true* D'Urberville, the last blossom in the tree. Sharon Tate, who had been raped at 17 but refused to let it scar her, well understood the cruel laws of life Hardy was dramatizing, and in Tess found a mirror image for the strength she had realized in herself. When she told Polanski of her experience, and her reaction, it made an indelible bond between them – a shared nerve where their comparably positive, forward-looking natures touched. To bring such a woman to life onscreen in Tate's wake would require an extraordinary actress, and by fortunate chance Polanski was convinced he had found one in Nastassja Kinski. Daughter of actor Klaus Kinski (*Aguirre, The Wrath of God* (1972)), she projected an aloofness, a loner quality indispensable to male screen presence, but riveting in a female. Polanski enlisted the aid of her mother and sent Kinski to England, to master not only English, but the Dorset accent.

Tess (1979) stands alongside *When Angels Fall* and *The Pianist* in revealing Polanski at his most humane. His sense of the absurd is no less present; there is, before all, that preacher indulging his "whim" in the film's first conversation. Yet this is sublimated throughout, in the service of a simplicity of heart. Polanski begins with a layered horizon, this time bedecked in wheaty gold. (A dedication reads, 'for Sharon'.) A phalanx of young women in white frocks and crowns of flowers cross to a May Day dance in a field, Tess (Kinski) emerging from their number. Her father (John Collin) follows, crossing the other way to his chat with the parson (Tony Church). Polanski's visual strategy is, as so often in the past, to hold the melodic note of each given shot. Here, and throughout *Tess*, he energizes such compositions from within by means of intricate choreography. Criss-crossing is constant, either by the characters or by his camera. One way or another (as in Hardy), a narrative and philosophical logic underlies such motion. People are either making choices, or choices are being made for them. When Tess arrives at the dairy farm owned by their namesakes, the palette becomes more varied, as do the means of conveyance. Tess' speedy carriage ride with the flirty Alec (Leigh Lawson) takes place in one setup, and the unblinking texture makes visible a spectrum of tensions which will propel the film, from here on. She rebuffs Alec, but one evening, feeling tired, she lets her guard down. He rapes her. Tess leaves and gives birth to his baby sometime

later, but it dies. No longer marriageable, she becomes an itinerant worker. After a time her still impressive beauty catches the eye of Angel Clare (Peter Firth), a parson's son who romanticizes her beyond reason as "a child of nature". She tries several times to be frank with him about her past but he either fails to hear the clues, or (in a particularly brutal mischance) fails to receive the confessional letter she has written him on the eve of their wedding. By the time he does learn the truth, they are already married and he coldly abandons her on their wedding night. Robert Towne has spoken with admiration of Polanski's confidence when asking an audience to wait. (He notes two scenes from *Chinatown*: Jake's 'hanging out' to the annoyance of a secretary, by way of forcing a confrontation; and his calculated baiting of the librarian at the Hall of Records.) "Roman's just not afraid to take his time," says Towne. "And the benefit for the movies he directs is that it makes everything that much more real." And so it is with *Tess*. The situation of a good woman betrayed by two men could have easily disintegrated into melodrama had Polanski not given his people the time and space to fully *be*. When Angel hears Tess' confession, his silence and his poise before reacting are allowed to become terrible. We can feel his response looming in his breath and body language, as we would in life.

Tess' downfall becomes inevitable once Angel has left her. She wanders a bit with her family. (They even visit the D'Urberville family crypt, and she movingly confronts the rows of marble effigies of knights, lying atop their burial vaults.) After several years pass, she decides at last to accept Alec D'Urberville's long-standing proposal of marriage, if only to keep her mother and sisters out of the gutter. Life with him proves miserable but she bears it, until Angel shows up one morning, begging forgiveness. (He manages somehow to be self-centred, even in this.) She sends him away. And yet seeing him triggers a depth of rage. After Alec cruelly mocks her tears she picks up a knife. The maid, hearing nothing of any argument upstairs, only sees Tess rushing down the steps and out of the front door. She then looks up, and notices a peculiar speck on the ceiling. At first it looks black. Then it turns red and spreads wide. *Blood*. It is seeping through the plaster from the upstairs bedroom, so there must be a lot of it. This is all we will ever know about Alec's death, but it is pulled off in an oddly comic, poetic style that one cannot resist. When the police catch up with Tess and Angel (who have reconciled), they are hiding at Stonehenge. She is fast asleep atop one of the ancient slabs, an angelic effigy of herself. She looks so peaceful that even the police are loath to wake her, but she tells them, "I am ready." They lead her from sight, into the layered horizons of the lovely landscape from which she once emerged.

Tess took nine months to shoot and twice that to find distribution in the US, where (to the astonishment of many) it was the most warmly received film of Polanski's career thus far, garnering box-office success, critical praise, awards and Oscar nominations in equally large measure. Many admirers gratefully read into Tess' misfortunes an apology by Polanski for his own transgression but he dismissed this. However stupid his lust in 1977, however mixed-up the fiasco with the girl, it was inconceivable, an insult to his sense of honour, that he of all people should ever *deliberately* victimize a female. His honest anguish at being so accused can be detected in his most defiant statements in the first months after his arrest. After all, his mother and Tate, the two women he loved most in his life, were victims of deliberate attackers. The most sympathetic characters in his art are always the victims, whether they are women (like Carol in *Repulsion*, Rosemary, Evelyn

ABOVE
On the set of 'Tess' (1979)
Cinematographer Geoffrey Unsworth (centre) did some of his best work on 'Tess', and was loved by the crew. He died suddenly, midway through filming, but was posthumously awarded a joint Oscar with Ghislain Cloquet, who replaced him.

OPPOSITE TOP
On the set of 'Tess' (1979)
Filming close-ups in the carriages was safe. Leigh Lawson remembers galloping the carriage downhill for the scene where Alec gives Tess a sexy fright. This is dangerous because the carriage can hit the horses and cause an accident, but Lawson did it. Since Polanski would never ask his actors to do anything he would not do himself, he then galloped the carriage down the hill himself.

OPPOSITE BOTTOM
On the set of 'Tess' (1979)
After she murders Alec, Tess and Angel go on the run. Polanski's austere rendition makes the moralistic Angel more of a monster than the caddish Alec.

Still from 'Tess' (1979)

Tess runs to join Angel by train. Her shocking red dress, which along with Alec's spilled blood is our first primary colour in a epic of muted tones, changes the pallet of the film, and sounds the alarm of her fate.

Mulwray) or 'female', cross-dressing men (like George in *Cul-de-Sac* or Trelkovsky in *The Tenant*). It is especially interesting in this light to consider *The Tenant* as a direct follow-up to *Chinatown*. By donning a dress, Polanski could explore those realms he was reaching for in Evelyn without having to fight Faye Dunaway. To understand his intentions in making *Tess*, one must take at face value its dedication 'for Sharon'. In its texture and epic span, which so fully sum up his career (as if he were conscious of reaching both a summit and a point of departure), the film could stand as a farewell, perhaps to film-making, certainly to everything Polanski had thought his life was about up to this point. In being 'for Sharon', *Tess* is at its depths an impassioned love letter to a no longer living recipient.

Polanski began referring to himself as a "former film-maker". He seriously questioned whether the ordeal of getting any film made was worth any more years of his life. He preferred to direct operas and act. For several years, he starred as Mozart in both the Polish and French stage productions of *Amadeus*. When he performed the play in Warsaw, he reconnected with old friends, retraced his steps in Kraków and Wysoka and committed his life story to paper. *Roman by Polanski* (1984) recounts his childhood, his fugitive years and schooling at Lodz, his ideas about art, his love for Sharon Tate, the aftermath of her murder, his unlawful sex with the teenager and the thinking, adventures and misadventures that went into his every film up to *Tess*. He seems blessed with total recall. His ability to evoke rooms, atmosphere, action and feeling are as potent on paper as they are on film. Yet the same limits apply. He hates to explain and refuses to interpret. 'Unreflective' was the

word used by one frustrated critic. Yet giving a reader the sights and scenes of his life, with 'reflections' only to the extent that they illuminate his or another person's motives in the moment, is in accord with his working principles as a film-maker.

One can only wish *Pirates* (1986) had fulfilled Polanski's original hopes for it. His autobiography attracted the necessary money from a Tunisian admirer, and despite his melancholy Polanski attacked this fresh chance with fire and commitment. There's not one lazy or compromised frame anywhere in the finished product. Stills from the film in progress show him scrambling up masts and commanding enormous crews via megaphone with his trademark exuberance. Walter Matthau, playing a role intended for Jack Nicholson, owns Captain Red and transforms himself down to the smallest details of his body language. One can only wish more directors had made the demands on Matthau that Polanski did. The Spanish galleon where most of the action takes place is a superbly wrought thing, authentic down to the pegs that hold it together. Sad to say, beyond such virtues, the film is weakly plotted and tedious. Captain Red may be a charming brute, Frog an ideal, idealistic foil but apart from stating their different positions, they never quarrel, which means they have nothing to reconcile, and we have no reason to root for either of them. Dolores, 'The Governor's Niece' (Charlotte Lewis), is an icon of exquisite period beauty and sings lovely madrigals, but otherwise she has little to do. She and the Frog are mutually attracted, much as Alfred and the innkeeper's daughter were in *The Fearless Vampire Killers*, but nothing comes of it. Alfred Hitchcock once said, "Suspense is only as strong as your story's villain." There is no villain in *Pirates*. Don

ABOVE
On the set of 'Pirates' (1986)
Walter Matthau, left, robed as Captain Thomas
Bartholomew Red, watches as Polanski, seated,
mimes the gnawing hunger he wants to see in
the film's opening scene.

RIGHT
On the set of 'Pirates' (1986)
Matthau performs as directed. 'Pirates' is
structurally identical to Polanski's early shorts,
'Two Men and a Wardrobe', 'The Fat and The
Lean' and 'Mammals'. Again, we have a power
struggle between Master and Slave, which is set
against the elements, in this case an ocean.

ABOVE
Still from 'Pirates' (1986)
The Frog (Cris Campion) is the latest in a long line of Polanski manservants faithfully indentured to bullying rogues. Captain Red has a notion to eat the boy, but The Frog spots a ship just in time.

LEFT
Still from 'Pirates' (1986)
When he conceived this film in 1975, Polanski originally intended to play The Frog himself, opposite Jack Nicholson as Captain Red. Walter Matthau nevertheless gives a superb, unheralded performance.

On the set of 'Pirates' (1986)
Rehearsing Red and Froggy's prison break, which will take place at night, amid a fireworks show of exuberant distractions.

Alfonso (Damien Thomas) is a stylish antagonist and has a fine swashbuckling moment when he turns the tables and takes his galleon back after Red has commandeered it, but this puts us in the odd position of rooting for him more than we have ever rooted for Red or the Frog.

A successful epilogue to Polanski's efforts is to be found (oddly enough) in Disney's *Pirates of the Caribbean* (2003). One cannot exactly cry plagiarism; Polanski so adored the legendary 'Pirates' ride at Disneyland that he rode it many times and even took Gérard Brach along in the early 1970s, by way of seeking inspiration. Clearly the makers of the Disney film were inspired in turn by Polanski. Johnny Depp's Jack Sparrow is a bright Xerox of Captain Red, Orlando Bloom's idealistic young swordsmith is an amplified version of the Frog, and the Governor's Daughter played by Keira Knightley is a feistier Dolores. The difference is that these characters are constantly making choices, selling each other out, then turning on a dime and joining forces at the eleventh hour. Moreover, the cadaverous villain played by Geoffrey Rush (and his menacing crew) drive the suspense very effectively. Yet the richness of period detail in the Disney film, its razor-edged sense of the absurd, so follow the trail blazed by Polanski that one cannot help feeling its makers committed *Pirates* to memory and asked themselves, 'How can we steal everything that's great about this, but turn it into a hit?'

ABOVE
Still from 'Pirates' (1986)
Red goes from ruling a ragged raft to becoming master of a stolen Spanish galleon. This being a Polanski film, we can only imagine he has another desolate little raft in his future.

LEFT
Still from 'Pirates' (1986)
We might complain that the story flags, or that not all the gags fly, but there is not a lazy frame in the film, or a performance that is not impeccably realized.

On the set of 'Pirates' (1986)
Polanski made the film in Tunisia, recreating the
16th-century Caribbean with a magician's relish.
Across the water one can make out the scale of
the sets, and the cleverness of the illusion.

"Billy Wilder once said, 'Did you ever hear of
someone saying, "Let's go to the Roxy, they're
playing a movie that was made within its
schedule?"' The Polish proverb is, 'The better you
make your bed, the longer you sleep.' There's
something in my character that appears to all my
financiers as something bad – which is that I care.
Whereas some other directors, the ones who give
up and yield to these attacks, do not care. The
other guys who make good films, as God is my
witness, go over budget as much as I do. Only
they don't feel bad about it. With me, it's a
trauma. I don't sleep. I'm sick, I'm tired, I'm a
nervous wreck..."

Roman Polanski

ABOVE
Still from 'Pirates' (1986)
On film, the illusion of a time and place is made seamless.

LEFT
Still from 'Pirates' (1986)
The Frog and Captain Red. What, or rather, whom, are they eating? For all that they fuss and feud, they cannot live without one another.

Journeyman
1987–1999

ABOVE
Still from 'Frantic' (1988)
A quiet corridor can be a thing of perfect menace. Dr Richard Walker (Harrison Ford) is puzzled that his wife stepped out "for just a minute" too many minutes ago.

PAGES 130/131
On the set of 'Frantic' (1988)
If you want to work with Roman Polanski, it helps to be in top physical condition.

Perhaps Polanski carried *Pirates* in his head for too long and it had worn such familiar, hope-filled grooves in his mind that he lost his objectivity. In any case, an American film producer named Thom Mount came to his rescue once the budget spiralled beyond the reach of the Tunisian money, and it was Mount who produced Polanski's next film.

Frantic (1988) is a Hitchcockian thriller which begins with a hero's sudden and inexplicable loss of his wife. This is a premise to which Polanski brings an unfortunate wealth of involuntary expertise, and the film's opening possesses a lifelike disquiet. Dr Richard Walker (Harrison Ford) and his wife Sondra (Betty Buckley) arrive in Paris at dawn and discover they have grabbed the wrong suitcase at the airport. Walker teases his wife, and takes a hot shower. She takes a phone call while he is under the spray. He emerges to find she has disappeared. He throws on some clothes and checks the lobby. (Polanski moulds some nice tense camerawork here as he does.) But she has gone. From what we saw of their affection, this makes no sense.

The hotel clerks are not impressed. The police even less so. 'Was she having an affair?' is the subtext of their every question. (This is, after all, Paris.) Even the staff at the American embassy patronize him. The world's maddening condescension adds a fresh torture to his deepening fear. Walker, thinking back, realizes the explanation for her disappearance is brutally simple and absurd: the luggage mix-up. He tears open the strange suitcase and its cache of clues lead him, first, to the corpse of a Parisian smuggler, then to Michelle (Emmanuelle Seigner), the dead smuggler's 'mule'. It was

132

On the set of 'Frantic' (1988)
Ford's charming spontaneity in the opening
scenes with Betty Buckley would seem to
originate in that mischievous look on his face, as
he and Polanski confer over the script.

her suitcase the Walkers picked up after she too hastily grabbed theirs. The mystery
item she ferried from the United States is unknown even to her. (We learn it was a
trigger for use in an atom bomb, coveted by a terror organization.) From this point
on, Michelle guides Walker through the mazes of the Paris underworld. One might
even describe *Frantic* as the myth of Orpheus (who navigated Hades to bring back
his wife), retold as an innocent-man-in-jeopardy thriller. Walker is so determined
that he refuses every invitation to doubt. This fascinates Michelle, who then
becomes such a convert to Walker's refusal of defeat that, in the end, she surprises
him, courageously taking a fatal bullet in the climactic shootout. This might have
been much stronger emotionally had she done so in a direct effort to save Walker's
wife, or to deny the terrorists their little gizmo, but her valorous nature is
nevertheless so memorably revealed that it haunts Walker and Sondra as they
embrace in a taxicab identical to the one where the story began, stuck in traffic
behind a comically enormous garbage truck. This positive outcome sets *Frantic* next
to *The Man Who Knew Too Much* (1955) and *Charade* (1963) but most of the film's
first critics held this against Polanski, as if even to excel in such an effort were
beneath him.

Well, hey, they cannot all be *Cul-de-Sac*. Stylistically, the opening cab ride into
Paris, with the highway surging at us from the vanishing point and Arabic radio
music filling our ears, is a moment of oddly effective foreboding. When Walker takes
his shower and his wife steps from sight, Polanski's camera moves in on cat's feet to
gaze at the empty space where she stood, while Walker melts from the frame, thus

Still from 'Frantic' (1988)
Walker's wife has evidently been abducted because of a switched suitcase. Michelle (Emmanuelle Seigner) has the item the terrorists are after, and volunteers to help Walker. A siren in siren red, she makes a play to seduce Walker, but he is resolute. He wants his wife. Michelle, impressed, becomes all the more fierce on his behalf.

preparing us for her disappearance and the world of harm he cannot see coming. Later, there is a dynamically imagined detour over a set of Paris rooftops. Powered by Seigner's witchy range of subtleties, Michelle woos Walker with a dance while they are in a disco, awaiting a promised breakthrough. She wriggles close to his chest like a serpentine curl of smoke, enveloping him in her sexual aura, yet he is oblivious. A mysterious little passage, this: she is testing the strength of his fidelity and he is passing the test, his eyes tigerishly scanning their surroundings, door by door and face by face. The more he ignores her, the more sensuous (and sincere) her exertions become, and it is out of this singular digression that her later bravery becomes not only logical but moving.

A transforming love entered Polanski's life with *Frantic*. He had found not only a muse but a soul-mate in Emmanuelle Seigner. For the first time since the death of Sharon Tate, he trusted both his own heart and that of someone else enough to make a life with her. Over the course of the next decade, they married and had two children. On film, their happiness has born strange but wildly funny fruit.

"[Polanski] *was the motor behind countless parties, at which he himself did not drink.*"

Janusz Morgenstern

ABOVE
Still from 'Frantic' (1988)
Michelle becomes Walker's initially demonic, ultimately angelic guide, helping him navigate the Parisian underworld.

PAGES 136/137
On the set of 'Frantic' (1988)
Rather than film the stunts with his actors on the rooftops of Paris, Polanski built a breathtakingly realistic set.

ABOVE
On the set of 'Frantic' (1988)
With that blast of light seeming to emanate from
one of his hands, Polanski could be stealing fire
from heaven, but no, he's just showing one of
the heavies how he wants him to die in the final
shootout.

RIGHT
On the set of 'Frantic' (1988)
Choreographing the final fight sequence.

On the set of 'Frantic' (1988)
Polanski, ever hands on, fires a gun as the camera rolls. Action!

Still from 'Frantic' (1988)
Michelle dies so that Walker can be with his wife (Betty Buckley). Polanski links the women visually through their red dresses. This is a recurrent poetic motif in Polanski's work. Red dresses figure in 'The Fearless Vampire Killers', 'Tess', 'Pirates' and 'The Ninth Gate'. The meanings vary as the stories do, yet the motif persists.

ABOVE
On the set of 'Bitter Moon' (1992)
Speaking of red dresses, here is yet another,
leading two moths to share a flame as Oscar
seduces and is seduced by Mimi (Emmanuelle
Seigner). Here Polanski substitutes his own
hand for Oscar's.

PAGES 142/143
On the set of 'Bitter Moon' (1992)
In the early part of their love story Oscar and
Mimi fulfil all the cliches of romantic melodrama.
In one scene, they even touch hands while
riding a swing ride. A special effects shot is used
for the close-up of the hands.

ABOVE
On the set of 'Bitter Moon' (1992)
The two are lovingly, even ideally paired at first.

"She gives you a hard-on, doesn't she?"

It is a moonlit night aboard a cruise ship to Istanbul. Oscar (Peter Coyote), a skeletal, flamboyant devil trapped in a wheelchair, has just posed this question to Nigel (Hugh Grant), a shy stranger openly mesmerized by the beauty of Oscar's mysterious wife, Mimi (Seigner). Nigel stammers, pleads innocent and when this fails, insists he is happily, or at least faithfully, married to Fiona (Kristin Scott Thomas). Oscar replies simply, "Cut the crap." It is evident to everyone who looks at Nigel and Fiona that their marriage is at a cold standstill. A witty Indian passenger (Victor Banerjee) has them pegged the instant he sees them together. Oscar can tell just by looking at Nigel alone. He does not mind that Nigel wants to make love to Mimi because he cannot function as a lover himself, being paralyzed. So as the boat steams toward Turkey and all aboard warm up for New Year's Eve, Oscar (a failed novelist) holds Nigel in thrall by spinning the intricate, semi-pornographic saga of how Mimi came to be his wife and how his sexual obsession with her landed him in a wheelchair. "Eternity for me," he grandly intones, "began one fall day on the 96 bus from Montparnasse to Porte des Lilas..."

Polanski, Brach and John Brownjohn based their script on a novel by Pascal Bruckner, and true to Polanski's poetics, *Bitter Moon* (1992) works equally well with the sound off, like a stealth classic of silent film. Yet the verbal fire of Oscar's non-stop flow of talk is one of the film's assets, a joy as performed by Peter Coyote. His prose is so iambically purple that we can guess why no one will publish Oscar, yet he is so spellbinding that we can understand why editors (like the one played by Stockard Channing) persist in encouraging him. His twisting tales of how he and Mimi fell in love, became soul-mates in sexual adventure, fell out of love, hurt each other mortally and then got back together constitute the one truly compelling story he has in him, and he is determined to make Nigel the vessel of it.

Nigel grows more besotted by Mimi with every steamy turn in these lurid confessions (which mesmerize him, despite his protests), and his own marriage veers for the rocks. "Anything you can do, I can do better," Fiona warns him. By New Year's Eve, both are poised to embark on affairs, Nigel with Mimi, Fiona with a handsome Italian, and with Oscar gleefully egging them on. Yet as the clock hits midnight, it is Fiona who, out of the blue, claims Mimi as her prize. The two women rule the dance floor with a sexualized tango that has the crowd whistling, as their husbands look on. For Nigel this twist is a desolation. For Oscar it is a fulfilment.

ABOVE
Still from 'Bitter Moon' (1992)
What lifts Oscar and Mimi's love story into giddy black stratospheres of irony and humour is that Oscar narrates their tale of decadence from a wheelchair, to the thoroughly appalled (but riveted) Fiona and Nigel (Kristin Scott Thomas and Hugh Grant).

LEFT
Still from 'Bitter Moon' (1992)
But as great as the mutual pleasure is, for Oscar (Peter Coyote) and Mimi the demand grows for stronger stimuli, wilder experiments, swiftly becoming darker and tipping into sadomasochism.

OPPOSITE TOP
Still from 'Bitter Moon' (1992)
Oscar and Mimi's story ends in tragedy. (Peter Coyote with pistol in foreground, Emmanuelle Seigner shot and dying, centre.) Fiona (in bed) and Nigel (out of shot) are left behind, as witnesses and survivors.

OPPOSITE BOTTOM LEFT
On the set of 'Bitter Moon' (1992)
Polanski prepares Seigner for her sexy, climactic dance with Kristin Scott Thomas.

OPPOSITE BOTTOM RIGHT
Still from 'Bitter Moon' (1992)
And the two women take it from there. Nigel thought Mimi was his to conquer, but a more profound game is afoot, one that may in the end propel him and Fiona to renew their marriage.

Has Oscar been planning this? Has he been laying a sadistic trap for this harmless couple? Nigel seems burning to ask as he pushes into the cabin where Fiona lies abed with Mimi. Oscar welcomes him in, remarks with a soft leer upon the beauty of both their wives as they lie sleeping. Then, his voice filling with emotion, he produces a pistol. He cries, "We were too greedy, baby," and shoots Mimi to death in her sleep, then turns the gun on himself. Later that same morning, Nigel and Fiona are left to shiver in each other's arms on the upper deck where we first met them, as the bodies of Mimi and Oscar are carried off by the ship's coroner. They have just stared into the abyss. Is their marriage over? They cling to each other as if in defiance of the question.

Throughout the story, Fiona and Nigel (who are bound for India) have made polite chitchat with a Sikh, a widower who teases them for believing that "inner serenity" or "marital therapy" are to be found in his native country. Midway, during a respite in Oscar's arias, the Sikh asks why Nigel and Fiona are childless, and introduces them to a living legacy of his late wife – their daughter, to whom he is devoted. It is Nigel who has resisted Fiona's wishes to have a child, and in this he is like Oscar, a man preferring at all costs to be the self-absorbed hero of his own life. Polanski is careful not to over-emphasize this theme. Oscar, Mimi, Nigel and Fiona are free to pursue their explorations guiltlessly, even irresponsibly, since that is their need. Yet when the smoke clears, the Sikh gentleman and his daughter are on the upper deck, regarding Fiona and Nigel with kindness and tact. "My father says to wish you a Happy New Year," the little girl tells them. Clearly, she is the angelic messenger of a more life-giving course than Oscar or Mimi could hope to navigate.

One compensation for all his hardships is that Polanski knows more than most people, firsthand, about the glories and perils of pursuing pleasure. So much so that, as an artist, he can stand apart from pleasure in the act of communicating it. The sequences in which Oscar courts Mimi, and she rocks his world sexually, are the most directly erotic moments Polanski has ever filmed, as well as the most romantic. These scenes are impossible to watch without strong feelings: delight, derision, even revulsion. Whatever one's own private response, Polanski's personal sexual and emotional investment remains no less private. He may be turned on, but then, maybe not. What lives on in the imagination is that Oscar and Mimi are blindingly aroused. We are inside their excitements, even if we do not share them. (Nevertheless, this movie is probably a hell of a lot funnier the more ticklish your sexual fantasy life.) Given his own rowdy history, one might assume Polanski would in some philosophical way side with the two wildcats against the poor square couple whose faith in each other is so savagely shaken. But (even if we ignore the admonitions of the Sikh gentleman) Nigel, Fiona and Mimi seem to possess their creator's most abiding sympathies – they all believe in love. Oscar does not. He uses the word but makes plain it means little to him. He believes in the pursuit of pleasure as an end in itself. If this does not quite damn him (there being no 'next' in Polanski's theology, only, as Mimi says "further"), it isolates him. "Have you ever truly idolized a woman??" he asks Nigel in fury, midway through their talks. Oscar idolizes love without being able to feel it, and that's a living form of damnation. As the seductive ambassador of pleasure for its own sake, he is a Prince of Darkness more terrifying, perhaps more actively dangerous, than any warlock in *Rosemary's Baby*, and his willpower brings him to a dead-end darker and lonelier than any described in *Cul-de-Sac*. With *Bitter Moon*, Polanski calls hedonism into question. In pulling the trigger, Oscar renounces it.

ABOVE
On the set of 'Bitter Moon' (1992)
Hugh Grant and Peter Coyote share a laugh
between takes, as Polanski listens in from under
the bedcovers.

RIGHT
On the set of 'Bitter Moon' (1992)
Polanski, who is seated at left to judge by the
energy of his posture, watches the video
playback.

OPPOSITE
On the set of 'Bitter Moon' (1992)
Filming the final scene, with Hugh Grant and
Kristin Scott Thomas. They have both tasted
enough treachery at each other's hands to have
need of mutual forgiveness. Their best hope is
that they know this, and embrace it.

TOP
Still from 'Death and the Maiden' (1994)
Paulina Escobar (Sigourney Weaver, right), at a concert with her husband Gerardo (Stuart Wilson), suffers private agonies when the orchestra plays Schubert's 'Death and the Maiden'.

ABOVE
Still from 'Death and the Maiden' (1994)
This is the very music a Doctor played as he raped and tortured Paulina when she was the blindfolded prisoner of a bygone junta. Might he be Dr Roberto Miranda (Ben Kingsley)? She is certain it is him, by his odd laugh, the scent of his skin and his habit of quoting Nietzsche.

On the set of 'Death and the Maiden' (1994)
Polanski and Weaver confer as they prepare one
of her earliest scenes in the film, a sequence in
which we get only hints of her inner torment.

Death and the Maiden (1995), Polanski's third outing with producer Thom
Mount, stands alongside *The Fat and the Lean*, *Chinatown* and *The Pianist* as a
rigorously political film. As with *Knife in the Water*, it is a 'chamber' piece restricted
to a single location and centred on three characters. The setting is an isolated
cottage along a rugged stretch of seacoast, in a nameless South American country
after the fall of a dictatorship. Paulina (Sigourney Weaver) is an outraged survivor of
the torture chambers of the previous regime. Her husband Gerardo (Stuart Wilson)
is a former revolutionary, now a minister of justice, and has just been appointed to
oversee the atrocity trials. This is a sore point, because he can only go after those
torturers who killed people. Whoever scarred Paulina will go unsought because she
is still alive, even though her ordeal made her unable to bear a child, damaged her

up. It is only Gerardo. He has had a flat tyre and has caught a ride with a doctor who lives in the region. The brief chat she overhears with this stranger makes her skin crawl but she puts that down to her fried nerves. Once the stranger is gone, she picks a quarrel with Gerardo over supper. Much of their back-story is artfully referenced here but never directly stated; the night is young. Things do not explode until after midnight. Dr Miranda (Ben Kingsley) pulls up to their door again on a flimsy pretext. Paulina, hearing his voice, recognizing his laughter, flees the house, stealing Miranda's car while he is inside chatting and tearing into the night. Gerardo is embarrassed, Miranda philosophical. The two men drink and laugh about how crazy women are, and Miranda (just making small talk? Pursuing an agenda?) draws Gerardo out about his newly-announced investigation, which has been all over the radio. He quotes Nietzsche. Not far away, along a grassy cliff, Paulina pokes among the Miranda's music tapes, finds *Death and the Maiden* and pushes his car into the sea. When she returns to the house, her husband is fast asleep in the bedroom and Miranda is asleep on the couch. She arms herself, draws close, sniffs his face and, satisfying herself she knows that smell, bashes him, gags him and ties him to a chair.

What follows treads a treacherous moral labyrinth. Gerardo, startled out of his sleep, pleads for Paulina to be reasonable. She could be wrong. The man's 'smell' is not exactly evidence that would hold up in court, and anyone could have *Death and the Maiden* among their tapes. Paulina is convinced. She has Miranda's snorting laugh down cold. She insists that she has *memorized* that scent and (amid a rapid-fire catalogue of his many vivid traits) mentions that her torturer liked to quote Nietzsche. The laughter and the Nietzsche both give Gerardo pause. Both are things he has noticed about Miranda. The doctor, for his part, howls for justice when they pull the gag from his mouth. Is he an innocent man, horribly wronged? He could be. His anguish is total and plays on Gerardo's fears. Or is he a crafty ex-torturer who

On the set of 'Death and the Maiden' (1994)
Somebody asked Sigourney Weaver if it was hard being the only woman on the set. "No," she replied, "It was hard being the tallest."

has read this situation and knows his only road to survival is to play these two off each other? Miranda tries on any number of voices and attitudes while pleading for his life, some vulgar to Paulina's sex. (Does that mean he is a torturer, or a repressed Latin macho flipping out in fear of his life?) The ambiguities hold, although as Gerardo puts Paulina's raw intensity together with Miranda's fishy denials, he is obliged to side with his wife. He urges Miranda to make a full confession, on Paulina's assurance that if he does, he will be set free and his 'case' will go no further.

Other troubles erupt. The new President calls to say he is sending Gerardo bodyguards who should arrive by daybreak. Miranda and Paulina keep reneging on their treaties. Gerardo assures her that Miranda's dodgy bits of semi-denial are exactly in keeping with what all torturers say, but Paulina is not interested in an 'official' confession. She wants to know the deeper truth. What goes through a man's mind when he does what was done to her? Why did he do what he did to her, in particular? Her agony is so total that it suddenly pierces Miranda and he becomes genuinely meek and submissive. They step outdoors, to the cliff over which she pushed his car. As the sunrise approaches, Miranda looks Paulina in the eyes and makes a profound confession. Nobody is writing down what he says. Nobody is taping him. He speaks straight from his heart to her. He speaks of what compelled him, speaks vividly of what he felt when raping her. What she looked like to him then, how her love of that piece of music singled her out to him. How he felt like God, being able to possess a woman from the inside, and "I didn't have to be *nice*," he says, spitting out the word. "I didn't have to *seduce*…!" His calm is so terrible, his compassion for her now so unstudied, that when he is finished, Paulina and Gerardo simply go home, leaving him there, kneeling, looking down at the rocks far below.

Is what he has told her true? Is he what he now so believably proclaims himself to be, a soul ashamed? Or is he an innocent man, miraculously channelling an unwritten Dostoevsky novel (all that Nietzsche coming in handy now), because he *is* innocent, and because her pain has so moved him that he knows the only way he will live is if he gives her this gift of a 'confession' she cannot otherwise have? Ben

Kingsley balances this man's inner reality on a knife edge that defies the gravity of an easily grasped motive. What he has told her is true whether he is guilty or not. Whoever tortured her, Miranda has accessed what was in his mind, perhaps because its truth is known to all males. Or? Perhaps he really is guilty. As Noah Cross told Jake Gittes, "Most people never have to face the fact that at the right time and right place, they're capable of anything."

Chinatown could ask for no truer sequel. *Death and the Maiden* ends with an extraordinary single shot. We return to the concert at which the story began. Once again, the music is Schubert's *Death and the Maiden*. We start close on a bass viol (just as we did in the first shot of the film), but instead of cutting immediately, as before, to Paulina suffering beside Gerardo, the camera now floats back, swinging around airborne to take in the multitude listening, letting us discover Paulina and Gerardo, and then moving in extremely close. Paulina notices someone above her, in the opera boxes. Without a cut, the camera floats up to find Dr Miranda, enjoying the music with his wife and two boys. He feels Paulina's gaze touch him. He turns, sees, and acknowledges her, his face expressionless but (for an instant) heavy-lidded with melancholy. Then just as quickly he meets the quizzical look of his young son with a flashing, fatherly grin and ruffles the boy's hair, listening afresh to the music. Still there are no cuts. Polanski's winged camera descends back to Gerardo, who discovers Miranda and scowls toward him before turning to Paulina. She has already abandoned herself to the music, to which she is again able to listen, albeit with a trembling will.

All the film's ambiguities are conjured and unified in this shot. If Miranda is innocent, then his sad look can be ascribed to the shameful treaty which gave him back his life, and the recognition that he has been the torture-victim *of* a torture-victim. And her anguished look toward him is likewise brimming with this possibility. If he is guilty, so much the worse, for they must now inhabit the same world, side by side, in peace, knowing what they know of one another. Countless human beings live in such fragile accord the world over. Former Nazis and holocaust survivors all too often cross the same streets, attend the same concerts, heed the same stoplights, raise families and lead lives. And so it is in with comparable former torturers and survivors in Spain, Rwanda and Afghanistan, no matter how law-abiding they have become in their respective old ages. Polanski at his most 'political' is neither academic, like Jean-Luc Godard, nor an advocate of choosing sides, like Gillo Pontecorvo or Costa-Gavras. He is an impartial student of politics in their essence, laying bare the idea that to be human is to suffer a terrible knowledge of the cruelty of other people, when young, only to face, in maturity, an even more terrible knowledge of one's own cruel capacities. His style is inseparable from such a meaning. The world which was laid out in fragments, in brief cuts, at the drama's beginning, is made visually and physically whole at the end. This unity has been earned the hard way, by what the people under scrutiny have been forced to reconcile in one another and themselves.

Still from 'Death and the Maiden' (1994)
Gerardo is his nation's Minister of Justice, now that the repressive dictatorship has been overthrown. His job is to bring torturers to justice. Is Dr Miranda such a man? He is not sure.

"You must understand. You have a certain goal when you make a movie. The goal is to materialize your idea of the film, which is somewhere visualized in your mind. At that moment, it's the cinema of one person, and I'm the only one who knows how to bring this vision into reality... When all of these people transform themselves into obstacles, I don't let them interfere with the route I'm taking. I can't."

Roman Polanski

ABOVE

On the set of 'Death and the Maiden' (1994)
Filming along the cliffside. Barriers have been
erected for the safety of cast and crew.

RIGHT

On the set of 'Death and the Maiden' (1994)
Because he is an actor, Polanski feels no
inhibitions about getting down on his knees with
the cast if need be and physically participating
with them in their rehearsals. For every scene,
Polanski first studies the actors to see what they
do, then he adds his own ideas, and finally he
designs the camera movements to capture that
performance.

On the set of 'Death and the Maiden' (1994)
Ben Kingsley dances at the edge of the abyss. It
is interesting to compare Dr Miranda to George
in 'Cul-de-Sac', played by Donald Pleasance.
Both men are highly strung but have a dark
machismo latent in them that can turn
monstrous. Both are put in jeopardy beside the
sea.

LEFT
On the set of 'Death and the Maiden' (1994)
Polanski, who has studied ballet, is probably a
choreographer at heart. Certainly, he thinks most
expressively in terms of movement and space,
which is one of the reasons his movies are
always so thrilling.

A far more playful shot opens his next film, *The Ninth Gate* (1999). Clearly, the myriad computer-driven revolutions of the 1990s enabled Polanski to achieve a dreamy mobility that would have been the envy of earlier film-makers, himself included, but here he uses these new tricks to maximum psychological effect. We fade in on an aristocratic old man surrounded by ancient books, at work on a letter. The floating camera takes him in, dips to eye a small leather footstool and then, without a cut, tilts up to reveal a hangman's noose. If we have any doubt about this old man's intentions, they are resolved in the next two shots: he seals the letter in an envelope; his slippered feet shuffle urgently across the room. Hitchcock held that if you show a person's feet in motion toward a goal but not their face, you are implying a sinister intention. Polanski cleaves to this and adds layers of his own. He shows the old man moving right to left, the direction of resistance, implying that his action will not only be sinister but difficult for him to choose. What is more, having shown us the footstool and the noose, the implication is comic in its directness; where else can such feet go? After this gentleman has dispatched himself, looping his docile head through the noose in one shot, the chandelier to which it is tied pulling loose in the next with a sparky shock, we move from his twitching feet and tilt as if on spreading wings, soaring across his wide desk and along the crowded canyon-rim of shelved leather-bound volumes filling the walls of his study. There is one dark gap in the whole row. A single book has evidently been removed from this collection. Polanski's camera eye swoops with a bat-swift turn into this dark gap. Thus begins a lively animated title sequence, his first since *The Fearless Vampire Killers*, in which we move across an otherworldly landscape through a series of spectral gates.

Without a word, Polanski has articulated for us a world where death is a literal stepping-off point and books are gateways into realms of both finite and infinite mystery. The missing item from the hanged man's shelf is a nearly extinct 16th-century text called *The Nine Gates to the Kingdom of Shadows*, believed by most of its owners to have been co-written by Lucifer. Dean Corso (Johnny Depp) is a crooked dealer in rare books who scoffs at the idea of Lucifer, Satan and witches.

ultra-wealthy employer, Boris Balkan (Frank Langella). Balkan has
copy of *The Nine Gates* from the dead man (he will not say how) and is
any price to have it authenticated. He even offers to let Corso carry the
g with him, tucked in his trusty scuffed shoulder-bag. Corso travels to
al and France to examine the other existing copies but finds himself in
nger. A book-dealing buddy (James Russo) is murdered, his corpse
risly imitation of an engraved figure in the book. Like the stumblebum
n Welles' *Mr Arkadin* (1955), everybody Corso comes into contact with
d, except for: Balkan, who may be behind the killings; Liana Telfer
widow of the elderly gent who hanged himself, and highly capable of
lf; and a mystery woman Corso calls 'Green Eyes' (Emmanuelle
) keeps intervening angelically (or is that demonically) whenever he is in
r.

nine puzzling engravings in the book. The female figure in the final
'I know now all shadows come from the light', bears an unmistakeable
to Green Eyes. Corso cannot help noticing, as he checks the other
exist, that there are creepy discrepancies. Each of the three volumes
e variants on the engravings, each signed 'LCF', presumably short for
n together, that makes nine engravings in the devil's own hand, a
deeply excites Balkan who is (by phone) shadowing his 'investment',
orso, all over Europe. By degrees, despite his ingrained scepticism,
nes fascinated by the reputed power he has in his hands. Not because he
ship or even summon the devil, as the engravings are purported to do
d in Depp's performance and Corso's deepening awe before Green
e he is a man tired of believing in nothing. Any evidence that there
re to life than just money and sudden death is going to compel his

Rafferty wittily described *The Ninth Gate* as 'a *Maltese Falcon* set in hell'.
frankly referred to the film as a light-hearted effort to tell an

entertaining story. Certainly the film (based on Arturo Pérez-Reverte's novel *El club Dumas*, 1993) demonstrates a sharpening of that ferocious attention to detail that has defined Polanski throughout his career. What he asks of his set and costume designers, of his camera operators, of himself, is that ever-elusive illusion of what Vladimir Nabokov called 'average reality'. He wants the illusion to hold, wherever our eyes fall. (This is why Polanski's films age so well.) So much that comes under our scrutiny is so solidly actual that even the most far-fetched plot twists (such as those invoking the devil) have lifelike weight and extension. Note the bold horizontal lines in the wall-decor at Boris Balkan's lecture hall. These are realistic details that become lines of force powering to the 'entrance' of Green Eyes into Corso's life, when he discovers her watching him. Consider too the subtle Chinese themes in the elegant decor of Liana Telfer's home. They add, with their layers of ceramic detail, a feeling of polished masquerade entirely appropriate to what this demonic priestess is going to impose on Corso throughout the film. Consider as well the wealth of potted plants, of little 'Thinker' and 'Reader' statues (most of them feminine) in the plush office belonging to the wheelchair-bound Baroness (Barbara Jefford). Such a galaxy of understated, atmospheric details reinforces the notion that somebody (indeed, a female) inhabits these offices, and moreover leads a life of the mind. (Peter Coyote, introducing *Bitter Moon* to an American premiere audience in 1993, told of how Polanski once spent an unusual amount of time adjusting an ashtray that was in the foreground of a particular shot. Coyote asked him, "Hey Roman, is this scene about two people or is it about an ashtray?" Polanski replied, "It's about everything that's in the shot. Everything we see has an impact on what we feel about what we're seeing.") The sets Dean Tavoularis created for *The Ninth Gate* are, like the lighting setups Gil Taylor and Ken Adam devised for Stanley Kubrick on *Dr Strangelove*, so fully realized that the director is given maximum flexibility of movement within a scene to extemporise fresh ideas and angles. Polanski is free to come in for a tight close-up or move out to an extremely wide shot (often in one sweeping setup), purely on the spur of inspiration, without fear of slowing his crew or puncturing the bubble of his patiently created dreamworld. The depth of his focus is not merely visual, either. Wojciech Kilar's music creates an aural carousel, circling and surging, as Corso is put through his paces. As Green Eyes reveals her true nature, the playfulness of the score gives way to heartrending beauty with the solo voice of soprano Sumi Jo expressing both isolation and communion in a single breath.

The climax of *The Ninth Gate* is twofold. First, there is the wild showdown at Leanna's chateau in the French countryside, where Boris Balkan boldly interrupts a witches' Sabbath hollering "Mumbo-jumbo, mumbo-jumbo". He then snatches his copy of *The Nine Gates* out of Leanna's hands. (She had earlier stole it from Corso and nearly killed him in so doing.) Balkan tells the hooded horde they are nothing but a pack of buffoons. "Buffoons!!!" He then murders Leanna before their panicked eyes, strangling her in such a showy way that the gold pentagram on her necklace crushes her throat. For an encore, he shouts "Boo!" at the mob, causing them to scatter. (Langella's wonderful buoyancy, whether killing people or toying with them, makes Balkan a rather cosmic tap-dancer.) Corso, watching from the wings, having stalked Leanna to her chateau to take back the book, tries to intervene as Balkan throttles her. Green Eyes stops him. To do so she literally descends from above, hurtling gracefully through the air. (She did this once before, in Paris, when Corso was being mugged by Leanna's henchman.) "Don't, Corso. Don't," she commands

ABOVE
Still from 'The Ninth Gate' (1999)
Boris Balkan sets himself on fire to make the devil appear.

OPPOSITE
Still from 'The Ninth Gate' (1999)
The body count escalates exponentially the closer Corso comes to unlocking the secret of the Satanic book Boris covets: 'The Nine Gates to the Kingdom of Shadows'.

(the first time she has ever addressed him by name). He accedes to her mysterious authority, watching her, as she watches Leanna's demise with the curious attention of one accepting a delivery.

Which brings us to the second climax. Throughout the film, Corso assumes Green Eyes is just a shadowy employee of Balkan's. What becomes more likely is that she is the devil everybody has been so hot to summon. She has been watching the proceedings all along, with a merry, indulgent fascination. The book everybody is so desperate to possess has only token value for her. She says mildly, "I like books." (She also says, "I like trains.") What really interests her is transport, be it in the form of books, trains, motorcycles, free-flying levitations or (as Corso discovers) sex. After Balkan is accidentally killed, having arrogantly set himself on fire in gleeful demonstration of the power of the nine engravings, Corso is half-smothered in a bout of highly spooky, otherworldly sex with Green Eyes, while the castle at her back is consumed with flames. Corso does not believe in the devil, which is why the devil has such a crush on him. This is one way to see it, at any rate. Another possibility is that, having no wish for power himself, merely an honest curiosity about whatever mystic realms there might be beyond the worldly magic of money, Corso reveals himself to be the devil's ideal mate. Perhaps with this intercourse he is also father to her offspring? *The Ninth Gate* constitutes a satisfying third in an unofficial trilogy that includes *The Fearless Vampire Killers* and *Rosemary's Baby*. Another way to see it is to turn all conventional notions of 'the devil' and 'God' upside down and to consider that Green Eyes may be Heaven's emissary and not

On the set of 'The Ninth Gate' (1999)
Polanski gives a wry Johnny Depp some grey hairs, a career first. He had played grown men before this (Ed Wood, Donnie Brasco), but Corso is the first Depp creation to touch middle age.

ABOVE
On the set of 'The Ninth Gate' (1999)
Emmanuelle Seigner, in real life Mrs Roman Polanski, gets physical with her director as they explore the combative set of movements he wants from Green Eyes.

LEFT
On the set of 'The Ninth Gate' (1999)
Polanski, clutching his baby son as he directs Depp and Lena Olin, doubles directorial and childcare duties.

Hell's, for she brings love into Corso's life. He is a changed man as he takes that final step.

In a world governed by absurdity, what else can love be but a devil? Given that Corso has the rare openness to seek love in such creative terms, how else can he be rewarded, except with a flash of light (however enigmatic) that removes him from this world? *The Ninth Gate* is the least appreciated, most richly ambiguous and most unjustly neglected of Polanski's best films.

Le temps retrouvé
2000–2003

ABOVE
On the set of 'The Pianist' (2002)
Revisiting these times would not be easy for
Polanski. He thinks hard while Adrien Brody
(right) awaits direction. Here again, as in so
many films, we will end where we began, in this
case with the hero at his piano, giving life
through his art.

PAGES 164/165
On the set of 'The Pianist' (2002)
Polanski lines up a shot of Wladyslaw Szpilman
(Adrien Brody). Polanski's bright red jacket is no
accident. On any production this huge, a
director needs to stand out in a crowd.

Around 1997, Polanski came across the memoirs of pianist Wladyslaw Szpilman, a Jewish man who lost his family to the Nazis but survived by moving from hiding-place to hiding-place as Warsaw was destroyed. His tale was harrowing yet upbeat, energetic, the opposite of heroic. He was repeatedly saved from death by chance interventions, either by admirers, resistance fighters or, in one haunting instance, by a Nazi officer. Szpilman wrote his account in 1946. Events were so fresh in his mind that he committed them to paper with an immediacy Polanski found thrilling. In Szpilman, he had discovered an alter ego ideal for mirroring that period as he experienced it, not as a victim, villain or saint, but as a flawed, lucky human being to whom this ordeal is entirely alien and undeserved. A survivor.

Polanski got together with playwright Ronald Harwood (*The Dresser*). They would talk through a sequence of scenes, Polanski pacing, acting, extemporising dialogue, after which Harwood would disappear to write while Polanski read over the previous day's pages. In this swift-moving manner, they emerged after six weeks with the shooting draft. Serendipity also governed the making of the film. The people of Warsaw gave the film crew an enthusiastic show of support and Polanski was blessed with cooperative backers who trusted him: "I wish every film I've made could have been done in such an atmosphere."

The Pianist (2002) brings Polanski's life and career full circle. He makes his own memories and formative experiences bear witness to an era, and calls upon every ounce of artistry and precision he has developed throughout his life. He never shows off. With a few deliberate exceptions, which are only to be found in those moments when the story moves through a major transition, the story is rendered in quick, razor-sharp scenes of less than a minute's duration. Periods of waiting, months and even half-years spent in fearful solitude (and Szpilman, played by Adrien Brody, certainly endured plenty of these) are rendered in this high tempo. The familiar tragic litany of 'ominous turns of the screw' Polanski describes in his memoirs are delivered here with fresh bite. The precise colour and design of the Star-of-David armbands the Nazis force their Jewish captives to wear (blue stencils against white, in exact dimensions dictated through the local newspaper) have the stinging vitality of things remembered, not borrowed from other films. The same holds for the odd tawny blond colour of the sandbags piled along the ghetto walls, the gun-metal grey of the street-cobbles, and the drab olive hues which feel subtly mixed with every other colour that comes under our scrutiny, even lemony summer skirts. If we happen to be ignorant that Polanski is a survivor and a witness to these events, the film has in its powers of persuasion the lively, disobedient jumpiness of Szpilman. As with Rosemary, as with Jake Gittes, he may not narrate, but we are inside his head from beginning to end. 'Witness' becomes the operative verb energizing the film.

Polanski's hand as a stylist becomes only briefly visible in a moment from which the characters cannot look away. As the Szpilmans sit down to dinner one night, a Gestapo raiding-party screeches to a halt in the street below. They rush into the house directly opposite, swarm up several flights of stairs and burst in on a family who are peacefully sitting down to dinner. They are a virtual mirror image of the Szpilmans. This poor group are attacked without mercy. Their elderly patriarch is lifted in his wheelchair and dumped out the window. The Szpilmans cry out as his body drops to the street with a sickening thud, and the Nazis mow the rest of the family down with machine guns. Polanski gives us this moment in one extended take, revealing the car as it pulls up, then panning upward through the house from

BELOW
On the set of 'The Pianist' (2002)
As the Jewish families await deportation, Polanski mimes a heartfelt direction to one woman in particular.

PAGES 168/169
Still from 'The Pianist' (2002)
A desolate scream. The injustices of an age are summed up in this image, without hope of catharsis.

Still from 'The Pianist' (2002)
Slave labourers are selected at random, and coldly killed, to lessen their ranks. Although Polanski has never filmed his childhood, what he saw and heard when young echoes throughout his work. As a boy he witnessed firsthand the spontaneous execution, by a Nazi officer, of an elderly woman in the streets of Kraków. He was later shot at himself, while hiding in the countryside at age 10, by a pair of idle soldiers who used him for target practice.

the Szpilman family's viewpoint as the killers noisily round the landings toward the top floor. The sense of anticipation is excruciating.

What he saw as a boy is reflected again and again in things Szpilman sees. The elderly lady that seven-year-old Polanski saw shot in the street has her counterpart in the young woman who tries to ask a polite question and is rebuffed with a bullet through her forehead. Similarly, a group of Jewish workmen are called out of the ranks during a roll call and ordered to lie on their faces, where they are casually shot to death, one by one. In such moments, when murder is so meekly awaited, and so meekly witnessed by others, one is hard pressed to know which is more horrifying. This sense of 'first-person eyewitness' is at its most painfully extreme when we look on with Szpilman at the famed Warsaw uprising, but can only make out those bits of the battle (most of them involving heroic rebels being gunned down) which spill into our field of vision courtesy of a broken windowpane. This is a non-heroic survival story, not for the sake of being perverse, or contrary, but to commit to film a hard truth once memorably expressed by another holocaust survivor, Bruno Bettelheim: 'Survival has little to do with what the prisoner does or does not do. For the overwhelming majority of [holocaust] victims, survival depends on being set free either by the powers who rule the camps or, what is much more reliable and desirable, by outside forces that destroy the concentration camp world by defeating those who rule it.' Szpilman is protected again and again by a force beyond his control: his talent. As passionate, as disciplined as he is in relation to his music, he has no control over the greatness of this gift, yet it is the one thing about him which not only defines his life, but in a mysterious way precedes it. He is literally pulled from the line as he is boarding the train to Auschwitz with his family, and why? Because the man sparing his life (a Jew who otherwise works in disgrace for the Nazis as a Kapo policing other Jews) loves his music. When he is working as a slave labourer in what remains of the ghetto, Szpilman's mates on the crew do not hesitate to help him slip away (it is the only hope he has of making it through the war), and others in the resistance are equally quick to set him up in a safe, secret

apartment. They too take a desperate hope in the music of which he is the custodian.

Polanski's ease in making close rooms feel infinite with menace pays off in those tense sequences when Szpilman is simply lying by himself on a bed, listening to the world go by. Likewise, his knack for action and his love for the absurd infuse a sequence in which Szpilman escapes a tank battle in the streets by stepping through a hole suddenly blasted in his wall, only to hang from the roof like a scrawny ancestor of Harrison Ford in *Frantic*. When Szpilman takes starving refuge in the shell of an abandoned house, two complex master shots accompany him. The first is a good scare: Szpilman chases a stubborn, sealed can of pickles that escapes his grasp and goes rolling across the floor, only to find it stopped at the booted feet of a Nazi officer. Polanski pans up, without a cut, to take in this man's face. This is in itself a humanizing gesture. Hosenfeld (Thomas Kretschmann) may be coldly poker-faced when we first discover him, yet the slow reveal anticipates a hope. The second such shot is a skipped heartbeat later, when this Nazi officer asks Szpilman to prove he is a pianist by playing something. It has now been years since Szpilman has touched a piano. The closest he has come was a poignant instance when he shared a room with a piano, and dreamily let his fingers feather the air above the keys, as he listened to the music in his head. Here Polanski and Brody (who is in real life a skilled pianist) together maintain the moment of breath-held silence to a point of dizzy-making tension. Szpilman's fingers never stumble, though over the next few minutes, they do become divinely limber. When Polanski finally cuts, it is to a close-up of a the Nazi officer. He is still outwardly impassive. Yet courtesy of Kretschmann's innate sensitivity, he seems transformed by an emotion whose name he cannot place. This is so low-key (a lesser director would have milked it into a tearjerker) that one is more moved remembering it than watching it the first time around. But that is as it should be. The same goes for that soft (but in hindsight, heartrending) moment when Szpilman and his sister are being herded toward the trains and he says to her, simply, "I wish I knew you better." That is how life works.

ABOVE
Still from 'The Pianist' (2002)
The children of an optimistic pamphleteer in the Jewish resistance are massacred along with their father and mother.

PAGES 172/173
Still from 'The Pianist' (2002)
Despair. Szpilman alone is spared from being sent to Auschwitz, solely because his genius as a musician is so prized by others that he is pulled from the train. Witnessing the wreckage all about him as he staggers away, he cannot justify his survival to himself.

Still from 'The Pianist' (2002)
When he chances across Szpilman in hiding, a hard Nazi officer Captain Wilm Hosenfeld (Thomas Kretschmann, right) softens just enough to ask Szpilman to play.

The transcendent moments feel uninflected the first time around but return to us as memory.

"What if I had had a marvellous childhood," Polanski once challenged Larry DuBois of *Playboy*, "with rows of lackeys and nannies bringing me hot chocolate, and chauffeurs driving me to the cinema? Then you would say I am that way because I had such a luxurious childhood. But the truth is I am just this way. Period."

It is fascinating to imagine what might have become of Polanski had his parents moved to New York in 1937, instead of to Kraków. With his outgoing nature and omnivorous curiosity, he might well have become a popular child radio star on the same timetable that favoured him in Poland. He might even have made a splash in the Hollywood of the 1950s. The studios would have had to rechristen him with a catchy American variant of his real name. We might know him as 'Raymond Polaris', that adorable runt who elbowed Sal Mineo out of the way at the audition and so romantically took a bullet for James Dean in *Rebel Without a Cause* (1955). (After all, he cut a comparable figure opposite the Polish James Dean, Zbigniew Cybulski, in Wajda's *A Generation*, made the same year.) Who knows, he might have stolen *The Graduate* from Dustin Hoffman, become a major star of the late 1960s, then graduated to directing just in time to do, say, *Downhill Racer* with Robert Redford. From there, *Chinatown* might have come right on destiny's original schedule. But then, if he had come by *Chinatown* in this all-American way, would he have fought

for that dark, ingenious ending? Can we so arbitrarily separate his gift from his experiences?

Two things are certain. Polanski's great talent is a natural force. One way or another, he would have arrived and we would be taking notice of him. Yet what he has known firsthand has so shaped and deepened him that one cannot separate his gift from his life's circumstances. The value of his contribution to the world, as a witness and survivor, has been profound, especially because his focus as an artist has always been away from himself, away from his private tragedies. This is, paradoxically, his greatness, because even his most escapist fancies have been grounded in life's hardest truths. Too many victims of history succumb to self-pity. Never Polanski. He fuses tragedy, farce, beauty and danger in ways so free of narcissistic self-regard that his art will continue to enrich and inspire others long after that unknowable future time, perhaps a century or two from now, when only the films shall be alive, and the extraordinary drama of his life story, which was always his and no one else's, is rightfully buried with him.

ABOVE
Still from 'The Pianist' (2002)
This astonishing, mostly wordless sequence is the most powerful in the film, and the moral epicentre of Polanski's art. For Szpilman keeps the whole wealth of human consciousness inside him, and releases it through the fingertips of his gift.

PAGES 176/177
Still from 'The Pianist' (2002)
An icon of ruin and isolation to match the final shot of 'Cul-de-Sac', with the all-important difference that this man continues to be headed somewhere. He has lost everything but his humanity.

Oliver Twist
2005

There is no space here for a detailed study, but if ever material were ripe for Polanski, *Oliver Twist* (2005) is it – the upbeat, heart-rending chronicle of an orphan who must venture through worlds of poverty, brutality, criminal fraternity, wild luck and absurd reversals of fortune, all by way of becoming... himself.

In Charles Dickens' novel, adapted in collaboration with writer Ronald Harwood, Polanski finds an ideal mirror for all his own great themes – loss, luck at love, the world's innate cruelty, optimism, courage. Barney Clark, playing Oliver, has an angelic, feral face in common with his director which expresses the inner life of Polanski's heart and imagination as fully as Adrian Brody, in *The Pianist,* embodied his outer, more worldly experience. Oliver's sympathetic shadow, the old man he might become if he is unlucky, is the crime lord Fagin (Ben Kingsley), a beautifully realized grotesque. Through him, Polanski creates moments which can pierce the heart – such as when Fagin thinks no one is looking, and croons for joy as he sorts through his horde of little treasures. Much later, he seizes Oliver in a final hug, as if grasping at life's meaning before it leaves him. He becomes a man impossible to judge, to mock, or despise and we are suddenly at one with Oliver's unprejudiced nature. Set *Oliver Twist* against Polanski's earlier work, and one can feel the artist deeply, more emotionally than ever, reconciling the man and boy in himself.

ABOVE
On the set of 'Oliver Twist' (2005)
Reproducing Dickensian London in Prague.
Note the green screen (centre background)
covering whatever evidence of our era intrudes,
which will be later masked with special effects.

Chronology

RIGHT
On the set of 'Knife in the Water' (1962)
Jakub Goldberg gives Polanski leg up, so he can
see what he is filming.

BELOW
On the set of 'Repulsion' (1965)
Originally, Carol murdered three people,
including Michael's wife who discovers the
previous two bodies. Polanski (wigged and wet
at left) played her death scene, but later cut the
scene when his trusted friend, composer
Bronislaw Kaper, pointed out that this killing was
too rationally motivated to fit Carol's pathology.

1933 Born 18 August in Paris, France.

1937 Moves to 9 Komarowskego in Kraków, Poland,
with family (father Ryszard, mother Bula Katz, sister
Annette).

1939–1940 1 September 1939: Nazis invade Poland.
Within a year of the occupation, Polanski and his Jewish
family move, first, to the Kazimierz neighbourhood of
Kraków (historically a safe haven), then later across the
Vistula River to a tiny ghetto prepared by the Nazis.

1943 Polanski's mother and sister are rounded up and
sent to Auschwitz. Days later, on 13 March 1943, amid
rumours that the ghetto is about to be liquidated, Polanski's
father walks the boy at dawn to the barbed-wire fence,
where he cuts the wires and tells him to run.

1943–1945 Polanski is a fugitive, from ages 9 to 13.
Although his parents have arranged for him to hide with
non-Jewish friends, the Nazi terror is so overwhelming
within the city that despite this help, young Polanski is
more or less on his own. Polanski's most stable hiding place
is the rural village of Wysoka, in the foothills of the Tatras
mountains, 50 km to the south of Kraków.

1945 After a chance encounter in the street with a
relative, he is reunited with his father, who has remarried.
His mother perished in Auschwitz; his sister Annette
emigrated to France. He resumes his education.

1946–1947 Aged 13, Polanski begins a professional
career as an actor, on the Communist-tinged radio soap-
opera, *The Merry Gang*. He later plays the title role in a
widely acclaimed play, *A Son of the Regiment*.

1948 Polanski is nearly murdered by Janusz Dziuba, a
young man who pretends to offer him a deal on a bicycle.
Only after Polanski narrowly survives this attack does
Dziuba confess to police that he has committed several such
killings, and is later executed.

1950 Polanski continues his education, first at the
Kraków school of Fine Arts (a happy experience, cut short
by a falling-out with an unstable, tyrannical faculty member)
and then receives his diploma from a lesser school in
Katowice. Makes his first screen appearance in the
apprentice film *Three Stories* (1951), a group work by several
young filmmakers then training at the Lodz Film School:
Andrzej Wajda, Antoni Bohdziewicz and cameraman Jerzy
Lipman.

1953 Plays a prominent role in *A Generation* (*Pokolenie*,
1953), the landmark film about Polish youth during the Nazi
occupation, directed by Andrzej Wajda.

1955–1959 Studies directing at the Polish National
Film School, makes 6 short films. (See Filmography.)

1960–1962 Marries and divorces first wife, actress
Barbara Kwiatkowska (aka Barbara Lass). During this two-
year marriage, as both their careers are launching, Polanski
straddles two worlds as a film-maker, directing his debut
feature *Knife in the Water* (*Nóz w wodzie*, 1962) in Poland,
while making a short *The Fat and the Lean* (*Le gros et le
maigre*, 1961) in France, with French backing, and *Mammals*
(*Ssaki*, 1962) in Poland, with the private backing of his
friend Wojtek Frykowski.

1963–1968 As *Knife in the Water* (nominated for an
Academy Award) is decried as "decadent" at home,
Polanski, newly divorced, uses his still-valid diplomatic
passport to emigrate once and for all to western Europe. He

LEFT
On the set of 'Macbeth' (1971)
The beastly burden of being a perfectionist. Polanski, shouldering star Jon Finch, momentarily takes the off-camera role of Macbeth's horse.

BELOW
Still from 'Chinatown' (1974)
Roman Polanski's most famous cameo is as 'Man with Knife', the dapper, pint-sized crook who cuts the hero's nose. A creature of pure menace, made immortal by a creator of pure mischief.

suffers episodes of poverty as he holds out for projects which sincerely interest him. Forms a lifelong creative partnership with screenwriter Gérard Brach. Together they cook up a horror script in a matter of days, which becomes the film *Repulsion* (1964). They trade on its success and ride a mostly upward curve: *Cul-de-Sac* (1966), *The Fearless Vampire Killers or: Pardon me, But Your Teeth are in My Neck (Dance of the Vampires*, 1967) and *Rosemary's Baby* (1968).

He meets actress Sharon Tate in 1966 while they collaborate on *The Fearless Vampire Killers*. They marry on 20 January 1968, an event widely covered in the world news media, because Tate and Polanski are considered leading lights in what was then the international jet set.

1969 Sharon Tate is murdered shortly after midnight on 9 August 1969, along with her unborn baby and several close friends (Jay Sebring, Abigail Folger, Wojtek Frykowski) and an unlucky passer-by (Steven Parent). For many months, the identity of their killer or killers is unknown. The firestorm of scandal and speculation in the press (most of it stupidly placing blame on the victims) leaves Polanski bitterly disgusted with the American news media.

1970–1976 Polanski recovers gradually. In 1974, he directs Alban Berg's opera *Lulu* in Spoleto, Italy. Whereas before he averaged one film per year, in the eight years after *Rosemary's Baby* he only makes four films.

1977 While preparing a photographic study of adolescent females for *French Vogue*, Polanski has a brief affair with one of his subjects, who he later finds out is under age. He is arrested. A fresh firestorm of scandal and publicity ensues. As Polanski admits in his memoirs, this time he had only himself to blame. He pleads guilty to "unlawful sex with a minor", and enters Chino, a maximum security prison, to undergo 90 days of psychological tests.

1978 After 45 days Polanski is released at the discretion of court psychiatrists. (He is judged to be neither a paedophile nor a pathological sex offender.) When Judge Laurence J. Rittenband suddenly reverses an earlier agreement and threatens him with "indefinite" prison time, followed by deportation, (actions later denounced by a higher California court), Polanski flees to Europe.

1979–1999 Polanski makes a life in Paris, directing *Tess* (1979), playing Mozart onstage in *Amadeus* (1980), and writing his autobiography, *Roman by Polanski* (1984). Between 1985 and 1999, he directs five feature films. He marries actress Emmanuelle Seigner in 1992, and as of this writing they have two children.

2002 *The Pianist* wins Academy Awards for Best Actor (Adrien Brody), Best Director (Polanski) and Best Screenplay (Ronald Harwood). Both the film and its awards serve to revive Polanski's commercial and critical reputation.

2003 Polanski announces that his next film will be an adaptation of *Oliver Twist*, by Charles Dickens. The classic novel is to be adapted by Ronald Harwood (who wrote the script for *The Pianist),* and is due for release in 2005.

"He armours himself against showing anything that might be construed as weakness... His aim is quite simply to be invulnerable, physically as well as psychologically – not the easiest of tasks, if you are only [five] inches above five feet tall, and not an ambition calculated to inspire universal affection... He has the necessary fitness of a hunted man, and he holds himself with the compact, aggressive tension of a crossbow. With either leg extended in front of him, he can do fifty full knee-bends on the other, and his stomach is like an iron shield. Tests of strength have an unfailing appeal for him."

Kenneth Tynan

Filmography

The Bicycle *(Rower, 1955, unfinished)*

Crew: *Director/Screenplay* Roman Polanski, *Cinematographer* Nikola Todorow, Panstwowa Wyzsza Szkola Filmowa (Polish Film Academy), Colour.

Cast: Adam Fiut, Roman Polanski.

The Bicycle, destroyed in a laboratory error, was intended to be a dramatization of Polanski's own near-death at the hands of a serial killer.

Murder *(Morderstwo, 1957)*

Crew: *Director/Screenplay* Roman Polanski, *Cinematographer* Nikola Todorow, Panstwowa Wyzsza Szkola Filmowa (Polish Film Academy), Silent, Black & White, 2 minutes.

Murder is a student exercise, a moody study of a midnight stabbing.

Teeth Smile *(Usmiech zebiczny, 1957)*

Crew: *Director/Screenplay* Roman Polanski, *Cinematographer* Henryk Kucharski, Panstwowa Wyzsza Szkola Filmowa (Polish Film Academy), Black & White, 2 minutes.

Cast: Nikola Todorow.

Teeth Smile, another student exercise, gives us a leering minute in the life of a peeping tom.

Breaking Up the Dance

(Rozbijemy zabawe, 1957)

Crew: *Director/Screenplay* Roman Polanski, *Cinematographers* Marek Nowicki, Andrzej Galinski, Panstwowa Wyzsza Szkola Filmowa (Polish Film Academy), Black & White, 8 minutes.

Breaking Up the Dance is the legendary 'documentary' in which delinquents crash a party. It was a prankish student exercise which nearly got Polanski expelled from the Lodz film school.

Two Men and a Wardrobe

(Dwaj ludzie z szafa, 1958)

Crew: *Director/Screenplay* Roman Polanski, *Cinematographer* Maciej Kijowski, *Music* Krzysztof Komeda, Panstwowa Wyzsza Szkola Filmowa (Polish Film Academy), Black & White, 15 minutes.

Cast: Jakub Goldberg, Henryk Kluba, Andrzej Kondratiuk, Barbara Kwiatkowska, Stanislaw Michalski, Roman Polanski.

Two Men and a Wardrobe, Polanski's first film for public consumption, is an absurdist allegory in which two clownish Everymen lug a bulky piece of furniture on an odyssey through an archetypal cruel world.

The Lamp *(Lampa, 1959)*

Crew: *Director/Screenplay* Roman Polanski, *Assistant* Adam Holender, *Music* Krzysztof Komeda, Panstwowa Wyzsza Szkola Filmowa (Polish Film Academy), Black & White, 7 minutes.

The Lamp is a brief poem centred on a fairytale toyshop whose mountains of dolls are consumed in a creepy mini-holocaust, triggered by a new electric fuse box.

When Angels Fall

(Gdy spadaja anioly, 1959)

Crew: *Director/Screenplay* Roman Polanski, *Cinematographer* Henryk Kucharski, *Music* Krzysztof Komeda, Panstwowa Wyzsza Szkola Filmowa (Polish Film Academy), Black & White/Colour, 21 minutes.

Cast: Barbara Kwiatkowska, Andrzej Kondratiuk, Henryk Kluba, Roman Polanski, Andrzej Kostenko.

When Angels Fall is an epic in miniature, lovingly rendered, in which the many decades of an elderly female lavatory attendant's life are compressed into the passionate memories of a single day.

The Fat and the Lean

(Le gros et le maigre, Gruby i chudy, 1961)

Crew: *Director/Screenplay* Roman Polanski, *Producer* Claude Joudioux (A.P.E.C), *Cinematographer* Jean-Michel Trzcinski, *Music* Krzysztof Komeda, Black & White, 15 minutes.

Cast: Andrzej Katelbach, Roman Polanski.

The Fat and the Lean, Polanski's first film in the west, is a short, two-character allegory about power and survival, palpably influenced by Samuel Beckett's *Endgame*.

Mammals *(Ssaki, 1962)*

Crew: *Director* Roman Polanski, *Screenplay* Andrzej Kondratiuk, Roman Polanski, *Producer* Wojtek Frykowski (Films Polski), *Cinematographer* Andrzej Kostenko, *Music* Krzysztof Komeda, Black & White, 10 minutes.

Cast: Henryk Kluba, Michal Zolnierkiewicz.

Mammals is a more buoyant, absurdist retake of the power-themes of *The Fat and the Lean*, exuberantly enacted, slapstick style, by two clowns with a sled, amid a universe of snow.

Knife in the Water *(Nóz w wodzie, 1962)*

Crew: *Director* Roman Polanski, *Screenplay* Jakub Goldberg, Roman Polanski, Jerzy Skolimowski, *Producer* Stanislaw Zylewicz (Films

The Fearless Vampire Killers or:
Pardon me, But Your Teeth are in My Neck
(Dance of the Vampires, 1967)
Crew: *Director* Roman Polanski, *Screenplay* Gérard Brach, Roman Polanski, *Producer* Gene Gutowski (Metro-Goldwyn-Mayer), *Cinematographer* Douglas Slocombe, *Editor* Alastair McIntyre, *Production Designer* Wilfrid Shingleton, *Costume Designer* Sophie Devine, *Music* Krzysztof Komeda, 124 minutes, USA original release time 108 minutes with cartoon prologue added.
Cast: Jack MacGowran (Professor Abronsius), Roman Polanski (Alfred), Alfie Bass (Shagal), Jessie Robins (Rebecca Shagal), Sharon Tate (Sarah Shagal), Ferdy Mayne (Count Von Krolock), Iain Quarrier (Herbert Von Krolock), Terry Downes (Koukol).
Although jinxed in its first American release, *The Fearless Vampire Killers* delightfully inaugurates the second, more cosmopolitan phase of Polanski's career by spinning a gothic fable about vampires bent on world conquest, and the sweet but naïve fools who hope to destroy them.

Rosemary's Baby *(1968)*
Crew: *Director/Screenplay* Roman Polanski, *Novel* Ira Levin, *Producers* Robert Evans, William Castle (Paramount Pictures), *Cinematographer* William Fraker, *Editors* Sam O'Steen, Bob Wyman, *Production Designer* Richard Sylbert, *Costume Designer* Anthea Sylbert, *Music* Krzysztof Komeda, 136 minutes.
Cast: Mia Farrow (Rosemary Woodhouse), John

Polski), *Cinematographer* Jerzy Lipman, *Editor* Halina Prugar-Ketting, *Music* Krzysztof Komeda, Black & White, 94 minutes.
Cast: Zygmunt Malanowicz (Young Boy), Leon Niemczyk (Andrzej), Jolanta Umecka (Krystyna).
Knife in the Water, Polanski's first feature, traces 24 hours in the life of a bored urban couple who take an attractive hitchhiker sailing with them, and use him as a pawn in their erotic power struggles.

River of Diamonds
(La Rivière de diamants, 1964)
Episode in the compilation film *Les plus belles escroqueries du monde* (*The Beautiful Swindlers*, 1964)
Crew: *Director* Roman Polanski, *Screenplay* Roman Polanski, Gérard Brach, *Producer* Peirre Roustang (Ulysse Productions, Primex Films), *Cinematographer* Jerzy Lipman, *Editor* Rita van Royen, *Music* Krzysztof Komeda, Black & White, 33 minutes.
Cast: Nicole Karen, Jan Teulings, Arnold Gelderman.
River of Diamonds, a short feature made as part of a French anthology, centres on an amoral, Louise Brooks-ish cutie fleecing a suitor in Amsterdam.

Repulsion *(1965)*
Crew: *Director* Roman Polanski, *Screenplay* Gérard Brach, Roman Polanski, David Stone (adaptation), *Producers* Tony Tenser, Michael Klinger, Gene Gutowski (Compton Films, Tekli Films), *Cinematographer* Gilbert Taylor, *Editor* Alastair McIntyre, *Art Direction* Seamus Flannery,

Music Chico Hamilton, Black & White, 104 minutes.
Cast: Catherine Deneuve (Carol), Ian Hendry (Michael), John Fraser (Colin), Yvonne Furneaux (Helen), Patrick Wymark (Landlord).
Repulsion, the story of a young beauty losing her mind in the isolation of her sister's flat, was devised formulaically as a horror film, to launch Polanski's western career, but it also comes up to his high standard as a genuinely personal, logical poetic nightmare.

Cul-de-Sac *(1966)*
Crew: *Director* Roman Polanski, *Screenplay* Gérard Brach, Roman Polanski, *Producers* Tony Tenser, Michael Klinger, Gene Gutowski (Compton Films, Teki Films), *Cinematographer* Gilbert Taylor, *Editor* Alastair McIntyre, *Production Designer* Voytek, *Music* Krzysztof Komeda, Black & White, 111 minutes.
Cast: Donald Pleasence (George), Françoise Dorléac (Teresa), Lionel Stander (Richard), Jack MacGowran (Albie), Iain Quarrier (Christopher), Geoffrey Sumner (Christopher's father), Renee Houston (Christopher's mother).
Cul-de-Sac is the summit of Polanski's first period of development as a film-maker, a tense, tragicomic masterpiece in which a nervous cuckold finds himself at the mercy of his domineering young wife and an American gangster when his island home is invaded at high tide.

189

Designer Richard Sylbert, *Costume Designer* Anthea Sylbert, *Music* Jerry Goldsmith, 130 minutes.

Cast: Jack Nicholson (Jake Gittes), Faye Dunaway (Evelyn Cross Mulwray), John Huston (Noah Cross), Perry Lopez (Lieutenant Lou Escobar), John Hillerman (Russ Yelburton), Darrell Zwerling (Hollis Mulwray), Diane Ladd (Ida Sessions), Roy Jenson (Claude Mulvihill), Roman Polanski (Man with Knife), Richard Bakalyan (Detective Loach), Joe Mantell (Lawrence Walsh), Bruce Glover (Duffy), James Hong (Kahn).

Jake Gittes, the stylish detective at the heart of *Chinatown*, finds himself dragooned into protecting an enigmatic, perhaps dangerous, perhaps heroic beauty from the clutches of her abusive but all-powerful father.

The Tenant *(Le locataire, 1976)*

Crew: *Director* Roman Polanski, *Screenplay* Gérard Brach, Roman Polanski, *Novel Le locataire chimérique* Roland Topor, *Producer* Andrew Braunsberg (Marianne Productions), *Cinematographer* Sven Nykvist, *Editor* Françoise Bonnot, *Production Designer* Pierre Guffroy, *Costume Designer* Jacques Schmidt, *Music* Phillipe Sarde, 126 minutes.

Cast: Roman Polanski (Trelkovsky), Isabelle Adjani (Stella), Melvyn Douglas (Monsieur Zy), Jo Van Fleet (Madame Dioz), Bernard Fresson (Scope), Lila Kedrova (Madame Gaderian).

In *The Tenant*, Trelkovsky, a shy, Kafkaesque nebbish, takes over a Paris apartment, only to find its previous tenant, a woman who committed suicide, has taken up ghostly residence in his head.

Tess *(1979)*

Crew: *Director* Roman Polanski, *Screenplay* Gérard Brach, John Brownjohn, Roman Polanski, *Novel Tess of the D'Urbervilles* Thomas Hardy, *Producers* Claude Berri, Timothy Burill (Remm Productions, Burill Productions), *Cinematographers* Ghislain Cloquet, Geoffrey Unsworth, *Editors* Alastair McIntyre, Tom Priestly, *Production Designer* Pierre Guffroy, *Costume Designer* Anthony Powell, *Music* Phillipe Sarde, 165 minutes.

Cast: Nastassja Kinski (Tess), Peter Firth (Angel Clare), Leigh Lawson (Alex d'Urberville), John Collin (Jack Durbeyfield), Tony Church (Tringham), Arielle Dombasle (Mercy Chant).

Tess traces the downcast fate of Thomas Hardy's vulnerable but stoic young heroine, whose life has been turned upside-down by the discovery that her dirt-poor family are descended from noble ancestors.

Pirates *(1986)*

Crew: *Director* Roman Polanski, *Screenplay* Gérard Brach, John Brownjohn, Roman Polanski, *Producer* Tarak Ben Ammar (Carthago Films), *Cinematographer* Witold Sobocinski, *Editors* Hervé de Luze, William Reynolds, *Production*

Cassavetes (Guy Woodhouse), Ruth Gordon (Minnie Castevet), Sidney Blackmer (Roman Castevet), Maurice Evans (Hutch), Ralph Bellamy (Dr Sapirstein), Victoria Vetri (Terry), Patsy Kelly (Laura-Louise), Elisha Cook Jr. (Mr Nicklas), Emmaline Henry (Elise Dunstan), Charles Grodin (Dr Hill).

Polanski's first (and hugely successful) Hollywood picture, *Rosemary's Baby*, is a supernatural thriller about a young woman who grows to suspect her husband and neighbours are devil-worshippers who conspire to steal her unborn child.

Macbeth *(1971)*

Crew: *Director* Roman Polanski, *Screenplay* Roman Polanski, Kenneth Tynan, *Play* William Shakespeare, *Producers* Hugh M. Hefner, Andrew Braunsberg (Playboy Production, Caliban Films),

Cinematographer Gilbert Taylor, *Editor* Alastair McIntyre, *Production Designer* Wilfrid Shingleton, *Costume Designer* Anthony Mendleson, *Music* The Third Ear Band, 140 minutes.

Cast: Jon Finch (Macbeth), Francesca Annis (Lady Mabeth), Martin Shaw (Banquo), Nicholas Selby (Duncan), John Stride (Ross), Stephen Chase (Malcolm), Paul Shelley (Donalbain), Terence Bayer (Macduff).

Shakespeare's tragedy *Macbeth* centres on a couple overwhelmed by demons of ambition they had not suspected in themselves.

What? *(1973)*

Crew: *Director* Roman Polanski, *Screenplay* Gérard Brach, Roman Polanski, *Producer* Carlo Ponti (C.C. Champion, Les Films Concordia, Dieter Geissler), *Cinematographer* Marcello Gatti, Giuseppe Ruzzolini, *Editor* Alastair McIntyre, *Production Designer* Aurelio Crugnola, *Costume Designer* Adriana Berselli, *Music* Beethoven, Schubert, Mozart, arranged by Claudio Gizzi, 112 minutes.

Cast: Marcello Mastroianni (Alex), Sydne Rome (Nancy), Hugh Griffith (Noblart), Henning Schlüter (Catone), Birgitta Nilsson (Naked Girl obscured by floppy sun-hat).

Lightweight, unpretentious, *What?* chronicles a weekend in the life of a Candide-like innocent who finds herself both clueless and clothes-less in a De Sade-like Riviera chateau.

Chinatown *(1974)*

Crew: *Director* Roman Polanski, *Screenplay* Robert Towne, *Producer* Robert Evans (Paramount Pictures), *Cinematographer* John Alonzo, *Editor* Sam O'Steen, *Production*

Designer Pierre Guffroy, *Costume Designer* Anthony Powell, *Music* Phillipe Sarde, 124 minutes.

Cast: Walter Matthau (Captain Thomas Bartholomew Red), Cris Campion (The Frog), Damien Thomas (Don Alfonso).

Pirates is an old (and alas, tired) project of which Polanski was fond. Walter Matthau is the scheming buccaneer Captain Red, who springs from his leaky raft to take over a Spanish Galleon, only to lose it again, all while in quest of a stolen Aztec throne.

Frantic *(1988)*

Crew: *Director* Roman Polanski, *Screenplay* Gérard Brach, Roman Polanski, *Producers* Tim Hampton, Thom Mount (Warner Bros.), *Cinematographer* Witold Sobocinski, *Editor* Sam O'Steen, *Production Designer* Pierre Guffroy, *Costume Designer* Anthony Powell, *Music* Ennio Morricone, 120 minutes.

Cast: Harrison Ford (Richard Walker), Emmanuelle Seigner (Michelle), Betty Buckley (Sondra Walker).

Although it owes a visible debt to Hitchcock, *Frantic* is a fine specimen of the 'innocent-man-in-jeopardy' thriller, in which an American doctor visiting Paris must navigate the city's underworld (detouring suspensefully across dizzyingly high rooftops) in search of his kidnapped wife.

Bitter Moon *(1992)*

Crew: *Director* Roman Polanski, *Screenplay* Gérard Brach, John Brownjohn, Roman Polanski, *Novel* Pascal Bruckner, *Producers* Roman Polanski, Alain Sarde (R.P Productions, Burrill Productions), *Cinematographer* Tonino Delli Colli, *Editor* Hervé de Luze, *Production Designers* Willy Holt, Gerard Viard, *Costume Designer* Jackie Budin, *Music* Vangelis, 138 minutes.

Cast: Hugh Grant (Nigel), Kristin Scott Thomas (Fiona), Emmanuelle Seigner (Mimi), Peter Coyote (Oscar), Victor Banerjee (Mr Singh), Sophie Patel (Amrita), Stockard Channing (Beverly).

A sexy, wildly funny, much underrated exploration of the joys (and limits) of the pursuits of pure pleasure, *Bitter Moon* finds Polanski returned to full strength as a film-maker, and constitutes a worthy thematic companion to both *Knife in the Water* and *Cul-de-Sac.*

Death and the Maiden *(1994)*

Crew: *Director* Roman Polanski, *Screenplay* Rafael Yglesias, Ariel Dorfman, *Play* Ariel Dorfman, *Producers* Thom Mount, Josh Kramer (Capitol Films, Mount/Kramer), *Cinematographer* Tonino Delli Colli, *Editor* Hervé de Luze, *Production Designer* Pierre Guffroy, *Costume Designer* Milena Canonero, *Music* Wojciech Kilar, 103 minutes.

Cast: Sigourney Weaver (Paulina Escobar), Ben Kingsley (Roberto Miranda), Stuart Wilson (Gerardo Escobar).

A chamber drama based on a play, *Death and the*

Maiden bravely refuses to 'open up' its action – staying focussed on a single night in the life of a South American torture victim, her lawyer/politician husband, and their unlucky houseguest, the doctor she believes to have been her chief torturer many years before.

The Ninth Gate *(1999)*

Crew: *Director* Roman Polanski, *Screenplay* John Brownjohn, Enrique Urbizu, Roman Polanski *Novel El club Dumas* Arturo Pérez-Reverte, *Producer:* Roman Polanski (Artisan Entertainment), *Cinematographer* Darius Khondji, *Editor* Hervé de Luze, *Production Designer* Dean Tavoularis, *Costume Designer* Anthony Powell, *Music* Wojciech Kilar, 133 minutes.

Cast: Johnny Depp (Dean Corso), Frank Langella (Boris Balkan), Lena Olin (Liana Telfer), Emmanuelle Seigner (The Girl), Barbara Jefford (Baroness Kessler), Jack Taylor (Victor Fargas).

In *The Ninth Gate*, a shady dealer in rare books finds himself in over his head among dead bodies and spectral enemies as he struggles to authenticate a demonic text called 'The Nine Gates to the Kingdom of Shadows'.

The Pianist *(2002)*

Crew: *Director* Roman Polanski, *Screenplay* Ronald Harwood, *Memoir Death of a City* Wladyslaw Szpilman, *Producers* Robert Benmussa, Roman Polanski, Alain Sarde (Canal+, Studio Babelsberg), *Co-Producer* Gene Gutowski, *Cinematographer* Pawel Edelman, *Editor* Hervé de Luze, *Production Designer* Allan Starski, *Costume Designer* Anna Sheppard, *Music* Wojciech Kilar, 148 minutes.

Cast: Adrien Brody (Wladyslaw Szpilman), Thomas Kretschmann (Captain Wilm Hosenfeld), Emilia Fox (Dorota), Ed Stoppard (Henryk), Maureen Lipman (Mother), Frank Finlay (Father), Julia Raynor (Regina).

Although Polanski remains in exile from the United States as of this writing, *The Pianist* in many ways concludes the third, 'wandering' phase of his career on a triumphant note – for the wartime adventures of Poland's master pianist Wladyslaw Szpilman provide Polanski with a vehicle to dramatize his own most primal (and historically vital) memories. With its Palme D'Or at Cannes and its several Oscars (among them Best Director), *The Pianist* has triumphantly restored Polanski to the critical and commercial mainstream.

Oliver Twist *(2005)*

Roman Polanski collaborated with the screenwriter of *The Pianist,* Ronald Harwood, to adapt Charles Dickens' novel.

Bibliography

Written by Roman Polanski

– *Roman by Polanski*. William Morrow, 1984.
– *Polanski par Polanski*, Boutang, Pierre-André (ed.). Chêne, 1986.

Interviews

– Cronin, Paul (ed.): *Roman Polanski Interviews*. University Press of Mississippi, 2004.
– DuBois, Larry: 'Playboy Interview with Roman Polanski'. *Playboy*, December 1971.
– Gelmis, Joseph: *The Film Director as Superstar*. Doubleday 1970.
– Rafferty, Terrence: 'The Fugitive'. *GQ*, March 2000.
– Tynan, Kenneth: 'Magnetic Pole: A Portrait of Polanski' in *The Sounds of Two Hands Clapping*. Holt, Rinehart and Winston, 1975.
– Weschler, Lawrence: 'Artist in Exile'. *The New Yorker*, 5 December 1994.

Biographies, Memoirs, Analysis

– Bettelheim, Bruno: *Surviving, and other essays*. Alfred A. Knopf, 1979.
– Bird, Daniel: *Roman Polanski*. Pocket Essentials, 2002.

– Bugliosi, Vincent & Gentry, Curt: *Helter Skelter – The True Story of the Manson Murders*. Norton, 1994.
– Butler, Ivan: *The Cinema of Roman Polanski*. A.S. Barnes & Co., 1970.
– Coates, Paul: *The Story of the Lost Reflection*. Verso, 1985.
– Goulding, Daniel J.: *Five Filmmakers: Tarkovsky, Forman, Polanski, Szabó, Makavejev*. Indiana University Press, 1994.
– Huston, John: *An Open Book*. Alfred A. Knopf, 1980.
– Kael, Pauline: *Deeper Into Movies*. Little, Brown, 1974.
– Katz, Ephraim: *The Film Encyclopedia*, HarperCollins, 1994.
– Kosinski, Jerzy: *The Painted Bird*. Pocket, 1966.
– Leaming, Barbara: *Polanski: The Film-maker as Voyeur*. Simon and Schuster, 1981.
– Malkiewicz, Kris: *Cinematography*. Van Nostrand Reinhold, 1973.
– Malkiewicz, Kris: *Film Lighting*. Prentice Hall, 1986.
– Parker, John: *Polanski*. Victor Gollancz/Villiers House, 1993.
– Salter, James: *Burning the Days*. Random House, 1997.
– Sloan, James Park: *Jerzy Kosinski*. Dutton, 1996.

– Thomson, David: *A Biographical Dictionary of Film*. Alfred A. Knopf, 2003.
– Wexman, Virginia Wright: *Roman Polanski*. Twayne, 1985.
– White, Alistair: *New Cinema in Eastern Europe*. Dutton, 1971.

Screenplays

– Polanski, Roman & Brach, Gérard: *Roman Polanski, Three Film Scripts – Cul-de-Sac, Repulsion, Knife in the Water*. Harper & Row, 1975.
– Polanski, Roman & Brach, Gérard: *Roman Polanski's What?*. Lorrimer, 1973.
– Towne, Robert: *Two Screenplays – Chinatown and The Last Detail*. Grove Press, 1997.

Acknowledgements

I am extremely grateful to Kris Malkiewicz and Adam Holendern, who shared their memories of Polanski when our paths crossed in Lodz, Poland, in December of 2003, as well as to Jerzy Wozniak, rector of Polanski's alma mater. Wozniak not only conducted a full tour of The Polish National Film, Television and Theatre School, but treated me to a screening of several of Polanski's early shorts, in the converted ballroom where they were first shown. Renaissance scholar and film-maker, Marek Zydowicz founded the annual CAMERIMAGE festival in Lodz, through whose offices I was able to make these connections.

My trip to Poland was sponsored by an arts-writing grant from The Sundance Institute, founded by Robert Redford. I'm grateful not only for this generous financial assistance, but the encouragement I've received time and again at Sundance from Jason Shinder, Amaya Cervino and Ken Brecher.

Boguslaw Kwapien, also known as "Bob of Bobtours.com", drove me from Kraków to Przytkowiece and then to Wysoka (see photo above), retracing Polanski's boyhood escape route from the ghetto and into the foothills of the Tatras. Bob's contribution to this book is immense. He acted as translator, charmed the locals and peppered them with questions until we were conducted to the spot where the Buchala family's little hovel had once stood. A

sharp-witted 90-year-old camp survivor (may he forgive me for not catching his name) kindly corrected the *rashomon* of confused directions we'd been receiving.

Kris Malkiewicz also made his rich archive of personal photographs available to us. Film-maker and scholar Paul Cronin (editor of the Polanski interview book cited in the bibliography) in turn shared his collection of virtually every news clip about Polanski that has appeared in English. Film Noir wizard Hubert Cornfield, a mutual friend of mine and Polanski's, helped Taschen make contact with the film-maker, in 2003.

Roman Polanski was not interviewed for this book, nor did he wish to be directly consulted. He has not sought approval of the text. The opinions, findings and analyses are mine alone. Yet it must be acknowledged that, in the search for photos and other visual materials, Polanski has been extremely gracious in allowing Taschen access to his personal archives.

Paul Duncan is my editor – patient, encouraging, indispensable.

A number of other debts are more difficult to quantify, though they are no less real. Robin Palanker, friend and artist, was the earliest of my fellow Polanski partisans, at CalArts in 1972 and after – we saw *Cul-de-Sac* for the first time together there. Robin introduced me to ballet maestro Stefan Wenta, a longtime friend of Polanski's. It was

through Stefan that I got to know Jerzy Skolimowski, Eva Piaskowska and other lights of L.A.'s thriving Polish community. The generosity and tough-mindedness of these many friends have afforded me a vivid sense not only of Polanski's roots, but of his loyal and giving personal nature.

Another great friend, director Michael Cimino, has over the years shared countless practical first-hand insights into the mind of a master director, among them his favourite quote from Polanski: "A great film is the result of all the compromises that were *not* made." Through Michael, I met composer Marek Zebrowski, who helps coordinate the CAMERIMAGE festival (at the right hand of that other Marek Z.), and who most decisively encouraged me to go to Lodz – in effect opening the floodgate to most the debts honoured above.

For many years, my buddy Lynn "Napoleon" Lascaro and I have made a ritual of seeing every new Polanski film when it opens. He and I fell out of that habit, and even fell out of touch, while I was working on this. My fault, entirely; perhaps I can amend that now. It is to Lynn Lascaro that this book is lovingly dedicated.

In addition, the editor would like to thank Isabelle Dassonville and Nathalie Radovic at Roman Polanski's office for their help in rooting out old and obscure images from his archives, and for their hospitality during his visit.